SIMPLE

Tips, tricks and insights to help you build,

TO

scale and sell your business

SUCCEED

SIMPLIFY

Tips, tricks and insights to help you build,

TO

scale and sell your business

SUCCEED

GARRY MANSELL

BROWN
DOG
BOOKS

Published under licence by Brown Dog Books and
The Self-Publishing Partnership Ltd, 10b Greenway Farm,
Bath Rd, Wick, nr. Bath BS30 5RL

www.selfpublishingpartnership.co.uk

ISBN printed book: 978-1-83952-453-0
ISBN e-book: 978-1-83952-454-7

Cover design by Kevin Rylands
Internal design by Andrew Easton

Printed and bound in the UK

This book is printed on FSC certified paper

I want to dedicate this book to my wife, Margaret. Not only has she spent over 40 years supporting me by doing far more of the stuff I should have been helping her with in our life together, but she has also been a sounding board and a provider of great insights as I struggled with decisions in my working life. When I left corporate life to go it alone she told me, 'When we were first together, we had very little, if we have to go back to that, such is life.' I can only hope that any of you who buy this book and dream of starting your own business have the kind of unwavering support that she has given me.

CONTENTS

INTRODUCTION

This book has been written for entrepreneurs, would be entrepreneurs, and for those people who are perhaps a couple of years into their new business venture and are looking for some advice, or perhaps even some encouragement. If this is you, then stand around in the bookshop for a while and read a couple of pieces that appeal to you, I won't tell anybody, it's what we entrepreneurs do. We bend the rules a little and try new things, we don't fit too well with the normal folks around us, and we find ways of getting things done that need a bit of creativity and sometimes bare-faced cheek. One guy who worked for me during my first career at Mars said to me, 'I'm like water, you tell me where you want me to get to and I will find a way.' He always did, and I rarely asked how he did it; he had every trait that an entrepreneur needed.

The book is a distillation of the work I have been doing in the last four years with several entrepreneurs and early-stage growth companies who I have been advising after the sale of my last company: an Anglo-Swedish software adventure that I shared with some of the smartest, funniest and most dedicated individuals I have ever known.

Anyway, I digress. What is contained in these pages are answers to the most common questions I have been asked, or the situations I have been confronted with, in the last four years of working as a non-executive director, board advisor and, in one case, Chairman with some cool new or early-stage businesses. The answers and direction I gave them, and have now written about in this book, have come from over forty years of work experience. Some of it spent in the corporate world, but most of it spent building, growing, developing and divesting new businesses.

This means that the book is not a comprehensive guide to starting up or running your business. There must be an 'idiot's guide' for that already, I have not looked. What it is, is my way of solving issues or creating opportunities. I have called it 'Simplify to Succeed' because that is what I believe in.

My mantra in business has always been, 'You know you will never have all the information and facts you think you need. Eighty per cent is good enough, and if you can't get that, make a decision anyway.' This makes you strip issues, situations and problems down to their component parts. It makes you simplify the problem and it helps you build simple solutions or actions.

I don't think business is hard. At the end of the day, what you are doing in a business is providing goods or a service that somebody, hopefully, wants to buy.

To do this you need to have enough money to invest in the start-up, you need to market what you are selling and sell it, you need to grow the business in order to survive, you need to be able to buy the things you need to make your business work, you need to be able to lead and take your team with you and eventually you need to get your business ready and dispose of it.

I have split the book into chapters that cover each of those aspects of business. You can dip in and out.

You don't have to read it cover to cover, you can skip parts, you can read the bits that interest you when you want to and, if you are still reading this introduction in the bookshop, look behind you. The sales assistant has their eyes on you. It's not a library you know, and it's simple: turn round, take out your debit card and make the bookshop and me a little bit happier. After all you have about 80 per cent of all the information you are going to get at this stage.

CHAPTER 1 – ON STARTING UP

When you are starting up, and your idea is burning holes in your brain, and you are finding it hard to sleep, this is the best time to start doing some real planning and preparing yourself for what is to come. This section will give you some advice about things like business strategies and why they are important. You will also gain some insights about how to raise the funds you will need and what investors look for when they are deciding where to place their money.

I'm also going to give you some advice about where and how to source those funds and just what kind of money you are looking for. Did you know there are at least two types of money: smart and dumb? Well, there are three if you include forged, but I would suggest that is not a sustainable business. The other piece of good news you will find in this section is the fact that you don't have to be the first one on the market with your idea to be a success.

What is a business strategy good for?

I was chatting to a friend the other day who was bemoaning the fact that the strategy of his business was not clear and therefore he, as a senior buyer in the organisation, often found himself out of step with the expectations of the shareholders and the board of his company.

Apart from suggesting that if he can't change this, he finds a new position, we got into the discussion of what a good business strategy is, how it is constructed and what it can do for an organisation. We had similar views, but they were different, and it reminded me of something another good friend of mine taught me a few years back when we were just starting Freight Traders, but more of that later. Like in all good stories the 'reveal' is at the end!

First, what do I think a 'business strategy' is?

Simply put, it is a course of action(s), aspirations, and decisions, originated and agreed upon by the senior executives of the business and the owners/shareholders. It is the roadmap that should result in the continuation of the business, hopefully whilst making a profit and generating cash and enabling you to meet or exceed customer needs. Remember, the first requirement of any company is that it should be able to continue to exist.

I am sure you will all have your own definitions, and you may well disagree with mine.

Having established a 'corporate' strategy, it must be clearly communicated throughout the business. Because, as you progress down the hierarchy of the company, people must make decisions, and they sure as hell should not have to ask their bosses again and again in order to make these. I still like the saying that was common in my old company Mars, Inc.: 'Ask for forgiveness, not for permission.'

The strategic plan, when well communicated and understood by your organisation (and remember, if communication doesn't work it is not the fault of the 'receiver' it's a failing of the 'transmitter'), will be interpreted at all levels.

At the business unit level, it will be the General

Managers who take the strategy and turn it into a series of plans, activities and budgets for their business. They will, with their own management team, build a roadmap of their own and, in turn, will be communicating these down to the operational level.

At the operational level, line managers work using the people and resources available to them to enact the business unit plans. Typically, this is where the functions such as manufacturing, marketing and sales, procurement, human resources, and all of the others sit and 'get stuff done'.

Again, I realise this is an oversimplification of the complex activities taking place in large organisations, but something like this happens every day all over the world.

So, these strategies all combine to tell us what we will do and help us ensure that we will not find ourselves 'off message' as my buyer friend often does. BUT a business strategy has another use... and that is for you to check the inevitable 'good ideas and new initiatives' that come along. You should always test these against your business strategy and if they are clearly not supportive of them your first reaction should be 'no, we are not doing that'.

Only when you have told yourself that should you even question if you do want to follow this new path, and you then must revise your business strategy to reflect this.

The truth is strategies must be living things. John Menzies changed from a UK high street retailer to one of the biggest ground handling companies at airports, and Mars entered the pet food business and became one of the largest in the field when, at the time, they were famed for candy. But I'm sure those moves either fitted with existing company strategies or were hard thought about before they were followed.

So, remember, your strategy has a hidden gift that you may not have properly realised or thought about. Not only does it tell you what you ARE going to do and how to do it... BUT it tells you what you are NOT going to do, and in doing so it helps to keep your organisation focussed.

Business strategies are not just for corporate behemoths though, every business, including start-ups, need to have a strategic plan and if you are just starting now, think about yours. It will keep you on track and it will help you explain to investors, new employees and everybody else that shows an interest in your business, including customers and suppliers, just what you are there to do. And not do.

Presenting to potential investors

As an investor in start-ups and early-stage growth companies I get to speak to many entrepreneurs. They vary in quality as you would expect, the ideas they have even more so. When people want me to invest in their business, or their business idea, I am looking for several things, and I am cautious with my money. After all, I worked hard to get it, and you don't get wealthy by giving it away. I want my money to work for me. I want you to show me that you are committed to creating value for my investment, hopefully by making yourself very wealthy indeed and providing me with a good and fair return for the faith I placed in you and/or the work I did with you.

I want to share with you what typical investors, me included, look for when reviewing your 'ask'.

Most of you will have considered, or will have produced, some form of 'pitch deck'. That bunch of PowerPoint slides you have worked so hard creating. It's usually that that I ask for and get to see after an initial discussion.

The fact is most people like to be told a story. The best start-up presentations take the viewer on a journey, they tell the story and map the path of the company and make the viewer want to be part of it. This is what you need to achieve.

The pitch decks I have seen and liked contain, as a bare minimum, the following. Test your own deck against this. If it comes up wanting, I suggest you change it.

- What is the business? Is it a marketplace, a product, a technology play? I want to know, set the scene for me.
- Why is it? Why now? What is the problem it's solving? Or what is the need it is fulfilling?
- Who is the target audience? How big is it now, and how big is it likely to be in the future?
- How is your product, service or solution different from your competitors, if they exist?
- What makes you unique? Your people, your approach, your technology, your product?
- Continue to tell me the story, what is your journey so far? Highlight success and failures, what did you learn?

- Describe your business model, how do you make your money?
- Remind me why I should invest. Let me know if there could be tax advantages to me, or other benefits from making an investment. Tell me how much you are trying to raise and against what valuation? Tell me why your company is worth that much now? Tell me why do you want me to be an investor? Is it my money, my skill set, my contacts? How much do you want me to be involved?
- How are you going to use this investment and how will you judge success?
- What are your growth plans? Prove to me you know your market and that the plans are credible.
- Show me the financials. I want to see your P&L, your cash flow projections and what indicators you are going to use to control your business and measure your success. I want to see both the history and the projections for the next two or three years. When will you be looking to raise funds again, how much, and against what valuation then?
- What have others in the market done? What is their growth strategy, do they acquire or grow organically, or both?
- Who is the team running the business and what governance do you have in place to make sure that decisions are collective? Show me the variances in the team, their history, and their skill sets... make me believe in them.
- What is your exit strategy, and when do you anticipate that happening? When can I get my

money and how much should I expect to gain for the risk I am taking?

Remember, I have probably looked you and your fellow founders up on LinkedIn already. I have probably looked at your history of previous company ownerships and directorships. I may have even trawled your Facebook and Twitter accounts. I will have certainly, at least, done some of my own investigation about the market you are trying to enter.

Be prepared to be challenged, be prepared to stand your ground, show your beliefs, be truthful and credible. If you don't know something, say so. Be prepared to come back to potential investors with answers. Remember, every interaction you get shows that potential investors are engaged with you; while you are talking you are getting closer to them opening their wallets, sharing their contacts, and you will be learning from people who have 'been there and done that'.

Even if, after you have done all this, you receive a 'no', ask why, use it to shape your story, to fill the gaps, to learn and get better. Remember a 'no' is only ever 'not now'. The potential investor you are talking to usually has an extensive network and making a connection with them is making a connection with their network. What is not right for them could well be right for one of their network. Don't be afraid to ask for help in that way even if they are not going to invest right now.

Funding your business

I often find myself talking to entrepreneurs going through some form of funding exercise. Sometimes it can be more of a crisis than an exercise. When it becomes a crisis I rarely dip into my own pocket, especially if I'm talking to someone I don't know well.

What I do hear very often during these conversations though is, 'I don't want to lose control of my business.' I fully support that sentiment, but that statement must be put in context, and must be evaluated against the need your business has for funds if you are the entrepreneur.

Firstly, if your business is so small, or in such trouble that there is a risk that you will lose overall control because you must exchange such a large piece of equity in it for funding, then I would suggest things have gone wrong much earlier in the business's life. This may not be your fault alone. Look at the impact the COVID-19 pandemic has had on many start-ups, which have often been last in the queue for government support in every country.

So, let's talk more about start-up or growth funding and the question people are really considering. Do I finance my business or give up equity in it? Let's consider that question.

There are many types of funding available to your business. I am going to consider the two options most people have heard of and have some access to: debt and equity.

If we consider debt funding first there are some common ways to find this, and they include:

- Overdraft. This is typically short-term funding arranged through your own bank. It tends to come with arrangement fees and a steep interest rate. It is most used to manage short-term cash flow issues in your business and can be withdrawn by the lender at any time, especially if, having provided it, the lender smells some problems with your business.
- Loan. This is longer term borrowing, at either a fixed or variable rate of interest repayable, normally, in monthly payments. You pay part of the sum borrowed and interest each month. Very often you pay more interest in the early stages of the loan term. Most people go to their own bank for this, but there are other options including specialist lenders, or peer to peer lenders, so it is worthwhile doing your homework to obtain the best deal. After all, you may be asked to secure a loan on any other assets you have, such as property. Interest rates are negotiable, never forget that point. Also, when considering loans, you may have friends or relatives who are willing to make you a formal loan at a much lower rate of interest than professional institutions.
- Trade Credit. If you are just starting, you may find your suppliers give you very little or no time to pay their bills. This, as everything, is negotiable. If you are better established and want to improve your cash flow, then you should try to negotiate improved terms with your suppliers (as long as prices stay the same, or only increase at a level that is better than you borrowing money from others). Most suppliers will give thirty, sixty or ninety days

for you to pay your invoices to them. One piece of advice I give all entrepreneurs is pay to those terms, not earlier, not later.

■ Credit Finance. Many banks and specialist providers will provide you with a business credit card. These often come with an interest free period, which could be around sixty days or more. After this, interest is then charged if you don't settle your bill in full and on time each month. This typically means that you have a further twenty-five days of interest free cash. But these cards often come with an annual fee and very high interest rates compared to secured loans.

■ Commercial Mortgage. This is a type of asset financing that typically involves you securing a loan on an asset such as your property. These types of commercial mortgages are often used to buy premises for your business, assuming you have decided not to lease or rent your location. Typically, commercial mortgages run over 25- or 30-year terms.

■ Asset Financing. Typically, these are arrangements with organisations that include deals such as leasing, hire purchase, sale and lease back, factoring, invoice financing and invoice discounting. In all these options you are typically borrowing money based upon either spreading the cost of buying something over a period, and the asset may or not become yours at the end of the term, or you are having an organisation give you cash faster than you would typically be paid by your clients in exchange for a percentage of the invoice value.

All the ways of funding your business, unless you are lucky enough to secure an interest-free loan, cost you money, but your share ownership is unchanged.

So, what are some of the ways to secure funds for your start-up or growth business that involve you exchanging some of your equity for funds?

- Friends and Family. This is typically the way that most businesses start. With friends or family exchanging their money for a few shares in your wonderful idea. This does not come without risk of course, to relationships very often. Incidentally, I would always advise you, if you use this source of funding, to ask the person you are entering into a deal with if they can truly afford to lose ALL of their money. It is likely to be the case, sadly.
- Business Angels. These are typically higher net worth individuals, often they have done what you are trying to do now. They look for ways to invest their money that have potentially higher returns in exchange for the risk they are taking. The risk is, of course, investing in you and your business, so be prepared for a lengthy discussion about just what share of your business they will get in exchange for their money. They will also want to know how you will deliver back to them a profit, and when.
- Crowd Funding. Several companies have come into existence in the last few years that will help you raise funds in exchange for equity. Typically, they attract very small investors who want to invest a few hundred, or perhaps a few thousand, in newer

businesses. The good ones help you value your business and manage the whole process, including helping you build your message to potential investors, but of course they do charge a fee for this, often based upon a fixed fee plus a percentage of the money you have raised through their websites.

- Venture Capital (VC) Firms. Rarely do these firms invest in businesses in their start-up phase. They look to buy into businesses that have some form of proven track record, and hopefully some sales. They typically look to invest when a business is trying to raise more than one million dollars, if not more. Different VC firms have strategies based upon the amount of the raise, or indeed the sector of the business. They will also discuss with you the value you are placing on your business and just how much of your business they will receive for their investment, amongst many other things that are too numerous to mention in a book of this size.

Now, let us get back to that comment I hear very often... 'I don't want to lose control of my business.'

The fact is money is rarely free, even bank robbers get caught most of the time! So how about you ask yourself the question, 'If I give up SOME control of my business, what am I getting for it?' followed by, 'How little of my business do I need to give up to get what I want?' and then, 'And what else can I get for it?'

Now you are starting to think in the right way.

If you don't have to give up any equity, by borrowing in an affordable manner, why should you?

I've always found the answer to that question is a simple one. It's because the people I am selling a part of my business to bring something else to me. Some expertise and experience maybe, or some valuable contacts, or potential sales.

Remember, they will almost certainly want you to succeed, because if you do, they get wealthier. It is in their interests to make their stake in your business work. But be prepared for them to want to help, to have opinions and to challenge yours.

In conclusion, the decision of how you fund your business is yours. The way you do it will have a lasting impact on your business in some way, whichever way you choose. Take the time to make the decision, research the options and make the decision in a cool and logical manner.

I can't advise you from afar, and this text is not intended to do that at all. You will find there are other types of funding available to you, including areas such as grants and government business loans, that I have not considered here. BUT perhaps I have made you realise that sometimes selling a small piece of your business to someone who brings something other than cash to you is not always the slippery path to disaster. Don't dismiss it out of hand.

The benefits of 'smart money'

I have seen many pitch decks and budding entrepreneurs in the last few years since I started to invest in start-ups. One of the questions I always ask is how much 'smart money' is in the business already.

For those of you who don't know the term, this is my simple definition:

'Money invested in your business by people who can add value to it in ways other than cash.'

I'm not saying that 'dumb money', yes, I do use that term openly, is a bad thing. It's just that that money relies solely on you to multiply it and might come with investors who consume your time and add little value. Some can be like vampires sucking the blood from your company and its people. In the early stages of your business, I would suggest you avoid the people with dumb money, especially when that money is so large that they can barely afford to invest it. Those individuals are likely to harass you and deflect you from your path. After all, if you had put everything you owned into a small start-up bank, wouldn't you want the people holding it to bring it out and show it to you once a week, count it in front of you, explain how it's getting bigger and then have them put it back in the vault... until next week! OK perverse example, but you get what I mean.

The other reason for making sure that you get 'smart money' first is that most of the people behind smart money have worked with individuals and firms like yours before. They know that growth isn't exponential, they know business plans and financial projections are 'informed guesses' and they are willing to ride the tiger with you. Remember, they are shareholders and as such they are protected by law, your dealings with them must be transparent, you cannot over communicate with smart investors, every communication is a chance to get some of the benefits of having them inside your business... and they want you to succeed. I told you this only a few pages earlier. They want you to exceed your projections. They want you to get wealthy because they share in your wealth.

So, what are the benefits I think smart money brings to your new business?

- Sector or Market Expertise: Smart investors typically are investing in your business because they see the need for your service or your goods. They are endorsing your thinking when you had your initial idea. They have insight. Think of the benefits of having someone working with you with twenty years of experience in the market you are trying to enter, and recognise they will have their own dogma about the market too. How often have you seen the entrepreneur on shows like Dragons' Den in the UK go with the 'dragon' who says, 'I know this market and I can...' Those are the entrepreneurs I bet on.

- People: Most smart investors have massive networks of individuals. They are the ones who say, 'I know just the person you are looking for', especially when you are looking for that hard to get individual that is in great demand. They also will probably help you convince that individual that they should be joining you and not some other firm.

- Challenges: Smart investors ask good questions, and often the simplest ones that you have not considered. They challenge your logic. They are the ones who say to you. 'So just how are you going to sell one bottle of mushroom ketchup to every man, woman and child in Russia every week?' when that is what your business plan is projecting.

- Buying: Smart investors are often investing in your business not just because it piques their interest, it's probable that they have been involved in your market before, they often know the suppliers of goods and services you need now or in the future. And they know the prices you should be paying.

- Mentoring: If this is your 'first rodeo' smart investors should act as your mentor. Educating and supporting you and your people. They should guide and support your decision-making whilst giving you the freedom to do what you do best, whatever that is.

- Finance: At some point, unless you are lucky enough to become rapidly self-funding, you will probably need to raise more money for your business plans. Smart investors may put more money in themselves at the appropriate time, but it is more likely they will be able to introduce you to other individuals and organisations that are more suited to securing you larger funds. It's clear that a business that has smart investors, with a history of success of their own and a record with several VC firms, will be able to help you secure your investment. After all, remember how hard it was to raise that first £200,000? Imagine what it is like when you want to raise £5 million or £20 million. You need friends with connections.

- Promoting: I'm not talking about buying adverts, I'm talking about these smart investors talking about your business to their own peers and connections. I have lost count of the number of times people have said to me, 'Well if you are invested, that is good enough for me.'

- Introductions: I knew you were all waiting for this one. It's true, the best smart investors can introduce you, via their network, to people you can sell to, people who are almost pre-selected. Those open doors you need to kick wide open. You want smart investors with big Rolodex's full of sales prospects that they will share with you. (For those of you under forty, a Rolodex is the manual version of your phone/Facebook/WhatsApp contacts list. I'm amazed you can still buy them!)

- Disposals: Smart investors are also usually very good at introducing you to people, organisations or businesses that will buy your business from you and thus let you live forever in the lap of luxury. Many will have taken businesses public. Most have been involved in good and bad disposals of companies and they know how the process works, who needs to be involved and how you must prepare your business for disposal. By the way, I'm a believer that you should not have to prepare your business for sale, you should run it so it's always ready to be sold.

In summary, smart money is always worth waiting for. Work hard to get it and secure it. Work hard to keep it and you will most likely get to the point where you successfully grow your business and get to a very happy disposal, or perhaps a public listing.

Crowdfunding your business

I have been asked a few times about my opinions on crowdfunding to raise finance for a business idea. Let me share my thoughts on this approach to fund raising with you, it won't take long.

At times I have become part of the herd and, through crowdfunding, I have given some of my cash to start-ups in exchange for some share in their business, four times to be precise. Of those I would consider one of them as now having a good chance of delivering a decent return for my investment. One is almost dead and the final two are pretty much in intensive care. I have only followed on with additional funding for the company that I consider has the best chance of success, so actually my experience as an investor in crowdfunding has been a bit worse than when I have been more engaged and involved in the investments I have made. This should not come as a surprise; my crowdfunded investments are all far lower than those I have made when I have been engaged directly by founders.

I decided before writing this to speak to some founders who have used some of the crowdfunding platforms that are in common use around the world, and their stories are consistent.

They tell me the major advantage they obtained from using a crowdfunding approach is that it introduced them to investors they didn't previously know, but many said this was a disadvantage too. Many of their new potential investors asked a lot of questions only the founders could answer. Whereas before they had been used to fielding questions from people who were investing tens of thousands of pounds or dollars in their previous ventures, now they had lots of people investing less than four-figure sums asking just as detailed a set of questions. Their workload to answer these enquiries increased massively compared to their previous funding attempts. It became clear that this was not 'easy money' coming in from very passive investors.

What crowdfunding does is open up share ownership and the potential of high multiples of return to investors who, in the past, would never have found a way to have this opportunity. In that way it is very beneficial. The fact that somebody can invest ten pounds in a company does make much more cash available to start-ups. Nowadays many crowdfunding platforms will hold these small investors' shares in a proxy manner, such that the platform is the conduit to and from the company that is gaining the funds, but it didn't used to be this way and companies found themselves with a very long list of very small shareholders. When you are just starting up, managing this kind of shareholder profile can make high demands on your administration burden as well.

Remember, good companies that secure additional funding are those that communicate regularly with their shareholders and, even if you do it via email, you must maintain that list. I am now seeing the threshold for entry for some of the crowdfunded listings increase. It is not uncommon for some crowdfunding attempts to include a minimum investment amount nowadays as a way of reducing the number of investors that must be managed.

Now, those may be a couple of the downsides of crowdfunding, but this reach does have some truly good benefits too, apart from introducing the company to new potential investors. Many have told me how the word of mouth generated and the general buzz set by crowdfunding investors on social media was a real benefit. In fact, your investors are marketing your goods or services for you, and a few of the people I spoke to who were using crowdfunding to help grow their business saw significant uplifts in their enquiries and sales once their crowdfunding campaign had launched.

But rarely does marketing come at no cost, and all the businesses talked about how crowdfunding is just the same as angel or early-stage funding. The same things must be done; the same rules apply. You cannot just put your business on a crowdfunding platform and expect people to come running to invest. The old saying is that if you make a better mousetrap, people will flock to buy it from you. In my view they will, once you have told them that it exists and shown them that it is better, and that you will be there to service their new mousetrap when it needs it.

So, what else should you expect to have to do if you are planning on crowdfunding your business?

Well, the answer is just the same as if you were trying to raise funding before the internet existed. You must prepare, plan, and talk about it. This means having documents that explain what your business is, expanding on its benefits and differentiators from the competition. You need to get your financials in order and show how you are going to use the funds. You will almost certainly want to create some content to do this and probably create a video that investors can watch. You will certainly need to explain what your go-to market strategy is and have a decent marketing plan in place. Remember, you are now competing for funds amongst a much wider group of competitors, and a much broader audience of potential investors. You must stand out, just like you always did.

Interestingly it seemed to me that, in talking to founders who had successfully met their targets for crowdfunding their business, there was something else they had in common. The early, more significant investments, for higher sums of money (five-figures and above), were normally obtained long before the crowdfunding campaign started by using the older method of talking to your contacts and network. These investors give credibility to your campaign because people are risk averse and want to invest in businesses that others have already committed to. It's the herd mentality you want to benefit from. You want investors to be thinking, 'Well those guys put a lot of money into this, it has to be a good opportunity.' So even when crowdfunding I would advise you to do the 'hard yards' before your business hits the crowdfunding platform. Do the work to secure one or two of these committed early-stage investors to act as the bedrock to your campaign that others will then join with and build on.

The other thing to recognise is that crowdfunding, because it is carried out on the internet, appears to be fast, but often it isn't. It is not just all the work you need to do to get your campaign ready, which may take months. When your funding round closes it may take weeks or even months to cement all the legal activities that must happen before you can start using funds, so plan in advance.

So, would I use crowdfunding for any new business I build in the future?

The answer in my case is a resounding no. But I would consider using crowdfunding for an early-stage business where I wanted to grow, and my earliest investors were perhaps now unable to provide the funds for me since the business probably needs bigger investment than the earliest investors have available. So, in that spot between having a business and looking for Venture Capital, I think crowdfunding has its place, but I would shop around hard for the platform I used to place my business.

I would want their fees to be realistic and their help to be expert. I would want to know they had access to a ready audience of committed, knowledgeable investors and I would certainly use them to help me value the business and 'dress it' for sale on their platform.

I would not crowdfund until I had a minimum viable product and a decent, if not comprehensive, social media presence and some sales under my belt. All these things add credibility to the pitch you are making on the crowdfunding website. I would certainly not want to crowdfund until I had secured those one or two major investors I spoke about, who were going to act as my bedrock in the campaign and who would commit as soon as the campaign became live.

I think these things give a crowdfunding campaign

a better chance of success, but I would only use it if all other approaches I had tried had not been successful.

I am sure those of you reading this will be able to quote examples of start-ups that have been massively successful by using crowdfunding from the start. As in all things in life we must make choices and take risks. I know where my decision would lie.

Venture Capital, should you take it?

It's time to talk about Venture Capital (VC), or as one of my friends described it to me once, in a way that was a little unfair, 'Vulture Capital'. It's also inaccurate, VC companies are very rarely found picking on the bones of a dead company, at least not as their primary way of doing business.

VC firms are in business, like all of us, with the aim of making a profit. They are in a high risk, high return business and so it is hardly surprising that they have a reputation for being hard and driven, and driving the businesses and the owners of those businesses they invest in hard. But you started your business realising that it was not going to be easy and' VC firms provide many things for you. At least the good ones do.

Apart from much needed funds to help you grow your business, they often bring a network of gifted and skilled individuals that they encourage you to work with. These people typically have built and disposed of successful businesses themselves and bring great expertise to your business. Often, they take a seat on your board as part of the conditions of the deal.

The best VC firms also introduce you to other

businesses in their network that will either be able to supply to you or buy from you, the two essentials of any business. You could also find them introducing you to potential partners who could help you sell the goods or services that you are delivering. For example, it is very common for a VC firm to help software businesses focus on their software, introducing you to implementation partners who can sell in, implement, and support your software to external clients while you continue to do what you do best, build exceptional software.

The other things VC firms do for you is introduce you to further sources of funds to fuel your increasing growth. Then when the time comes to launch an Initial Public Offering (IPO) or sell your business to realise its value, and have you running off to the superyacht salesman to go and buy your status symbol, well, few companies can do this without the services of a VC firm.

So, this all sounds wonderful, doesn't it? It can be, but it comes with a price.

You all already know that the VC firm is going to exchange the funds and time it invests in you for shares in your business. It will try and get as big a share as it can for the minimum amount of investment that suits its view of the business plan you have. Note I say its view, not yours. There is something beneficial here though. For the first time you are likely to have somebody, in the shape of the VC firm, valuing your business. If you have previously had some angel investors you will be able to demonstrate to them just how much value you have created for them. But you are still a long way from manifesting this value for them as returns, and now you are going to be issuing more shares and probably diluting their holding as a result of this unless they follow on and match the VC firm's investment to keep their relative percentage share in your business. It also dilutes your share ownership of course. But, as I have often said to owners, 'What would you rather have, 1 per cent of a business worth one hundred million or 10 per cent of a business worth five million?' Dilution is not always bad, but loss of control can be hard to take if that happens at the same time.

VC firms often like to exchange their money for 'convertible preference shares'. These are a special type of share in your business that give the holders some additional benefits, especially if the business fails. This type of share typically has voting rights and it also gives the holder of the shares the right to convert their shares to ordinary shares at their discretion. These shares often give the holders the rights to cumulative dividends that must be paid to them before dividends are paid to ordinary shareholders. The other benefit of these shares is that, should the business fail, holders of these preferred shares stand ahead of ordinary shareholders in the event of your company being liquidated.

When you consider that about one in fifteen companies that VC firms invest in results in a large 'pay day' for them, and the rest result in them losing a significant part of their investment, despite having preference shares, it's hardly a surprise that they want to minimise the high risks they are taking in the shape of high rewards.

Now, if you are still interested in talking to VC firms

and gaining funding from them, I have another word of caution. If you are a start-up your chances of gaining funding from a VC firm are very small. I am led to believe by my friends in VC firms that less than 1 per cent of start-up companies get VC funding. VC firms tend to specialise in either industry sectors or sizes of companies. It's why you will often hear them talking about focussing on 'FinTech' or some other hot sector. Or you will find that they are willing to speak only to companies that have already got a well-established business with revenues greater than a specific number of millions.

One thing is common amongst VC firms though. They place greater faith in the demonstration of a competent, balanced management team than they do in a wonderful business idea. The fact is, people who have already shown success in working with VC firms to build and divest businesses that deliver against their promises are far more likely to gain new funding from VC firms for other businesses. It's one of the reasons I spoke about you looking for angel investors that bring your start-up 'smart money' when you select them. If you find an angel with funds, expertise in your sector and a proven record in working with VC firms, I suggest you hold onto them and listen to their advice, especially about the valuation you are placing on your business.

My feeling is VC firms are very valuable at the right time in your business life, and that is when you are established and are looking to grow. You will probably be looking to expand your sales and marketing efforts or invest in new premises or manufacturing processes.

But talking to them is a negotiation. They want to minimise their risk in what is a high-risk environment, and they do this in many of the ways I have talked about. In selecting a VC firm make sure that there are no other funds available to you for your plans, that the firm and its people are right for you and that they can genuinely bring you something more than money.

Sweat equity is the answer

I have been asked several times, what about using 'sweat equity' in start-ups or early-stage growth businesses. I have also been asked to be part of this type of agreement several times.

I am now going to share with you the pros and cons of this, in my opinion, for those on both sides of the coin.

First, for those of you who don't already know what I mean by 'sweat equity', it is where someone works for a company for no salary, but in exchange for their effort and expertise they get a share of the company, some equity.

Next let me make it clear. I am not talking about those people I consider to be the founders of a business. It is very common that those folks, the people who get together and have the idea in the first place, or start to develop it, rarely take a salary from the business at first. For them it's all sweat and all the equity. I'm talking here about when you, as the founders, discover the gaps in your experience, knowledge or capability and start to engage more people either on a full-time or part time basis. Your first round of employees. When you probably still don't have enough money to pay salaries.

So as a founder, what are the pros of employing people using sweat equity?

First, of course, it doesn't cost you any cash. We all know how precious cash is to a business. So, having somebody work in the business and not draw a salary but get a piece of the business sounds very attractive. In fact, it should make the individual more committed to help the business grow and become profitable because that is how they get their reward. If you can get people to do this, it's a 'no brainer' isn't it? After all you will only be giving them a small share of the business and you have lots of it left, don't you?

Another advantage for you as a founder is that the kind of people who can do this are often financially independent and often have far more experience than you in specific functions of business. Maybe it's sales and marketing, or manufacturing. At least it should be something that is not your strength or else you wouldn't be looking for their help, would you?

Truly though, that is where I see the major advantages for you as a founder start to dry up. In the excitement of the start-up and growth phases of your business it can be a quick fix and you forget the issues it can cause, especially if you don't pay attention to the details of the sweat equity arrangement.

So, let's talk about the cons of using sweat equity, just what are they?

Well first it is not free. It may feel that way, but it is costing you part of your business. I always advise founders to keep as much of their business as they can in the early stages and only start to trade shares in it when it has a proven value. Business values can grow very quickly in their early years, assuming you have some form of success. You will be amazed how much more your business becomes worth when you record your first sales, for example. I have lost count of the number of founders who tell me that they feel they have 'given away' too much of their business in their early days.

Next, even if you do find a very useful employee, or perhaps make them a director, who works for sweat equity, they do have to survive. If the person does not have an independent source of money, they will at some point need to get paid. At that stage you could lose them or must pay them at least a rudimentary salary. The odds are it is going to take you longer to generate cash from sales in your business than your business plan suggested when you convinced the person to work with you. So be prepared for that.

Another thing to consider is that most people working for sweat equity, either those who have made their fortune already or those who need to provide for their own needs normally, are not going to be working for you and you alone. Most have other interests as well, so you can often find that things take longer to happen than you would like, and for start-ups that can prove terminal.

Now I have touched on the subject of losing your sweat equity employee, it seems like it would be a good time to mention the details of the sweat equity agreement you didn't quite get round to formalising with them. They leave your business and they take their shares in your business with them, if there wasn't something in your agreement that managed this situation. Stop laughing as you read this, I know you would never be that stupid, but I know lots of founders who were.

Since I am now talking about the agreement you make with them when they sign up, let me share with you the most common mistake I see made in this area. It is in the field of sales.

I have lost count of the number of times I have heard a founder tell me that they have a great person engaged, working for sweat equity, who has a wonderful network of contacts, are fabulous communicators, really understand what the business is offering and will make introductions for us in exchange for equity. You will be amazed how many people there are like this in the business world, and how many of them have shares in dead companies that they have 'helped' in this way.

Introductions and referrals are often the lifeblood of start-ups, you need these people, but when you engage with them make sure your agreement with them is based on the value they provide and deliver. Make sure you have something in writing that says, 'I am going to give you X per cent of the business in exchange for you delivering Y millions of invoiced and paid for sales.' By all means have this staged or give them shares that vest and thus come into their ownership only when these conditions have been met over a defined period of time.

Another area of difficulty I have seen with sweat equity is trying to agree on just how much the equity and the person's time is worth. Just how do you decide on how many shares they get for the work they do?

Sadly, there is no right answer, it is a negotiation between you and the person. You may have some clues if you have already received some angel investment because you and your investors will, at that point, have agreed what the company is worth. But it will have been at that point in time. Company values can and do go up and down. In reaching this agreement with the person, be brutally honest about what they are and what they bring to your business. Use your business plan to help you. It will estimate what your company is going to be worth in two years' time for example.

When evaluating the person, think about how much you would be willing to pay for a person in your company as a full-time employee like them at that time. Are they really your sales director (for example) in that business? If they are, then make sure you give them a deal that at least matches the rewards you would be paying for a sales director for the two years it has taken to build your business to the point where it needs one, and then add a premium to it for the risk they are taking in not being paid a salary for two years.

Any way you do this, make sure that you protect yourself and your business from what could be a very messy divorce if things do not work out. There are many ways you can do this, using buy-back clauses or vesting for example, but do not fail to do it.

So, would I use sweat equity for early employees? My answer is no, but I would incentivise them with some form of company ownership. I have often used things like share options in exchange for a reduced salary. Vesting I have also used. In a few businesses I have used a clause in contracts that guarantee them a payment equivalent to a percentage of the company when it is sold, assuming they are still employed by the company.

It is also not uncommon to use company equity as a 'Golden Hello' for a key appointment. For example, giving 5 per cent of the business to a new CEO, along with a reduced salary, is quite common, assuming you protect yourself against that messy divorce if it doesn't work out. I have even given the option to buy shares in a company at a reduced price to key suppliers in exchange for lower cost services or materials that the business needed.

You can be creative if you operate inside the laws of your country in all these dealings, but always make sure that arrangements are clear, transparent and in writing.

As for those people with the great networks who guarantee you sales that I talked about earlier. Well, I would always suggest paying them on a commission basis in cold hard cash, not equity. You can always offer to exchange that cash for shares in your company if you want to!

Last mover advantage

So why are some fast-growth tech companies that haven't made a profit worth so much?

The valuation of most companies is pretty much directly tied to just how much cash they are generating or, more importantly, how much cash they will generate in their lifetime. One way of looking at this is to value a company by estimating the sum of all the money it will make in the future. You need to discount the future money of course, since money in your hand now is worth more than money you don't yet have. This is the basis of a discounted cash flow valuation.

Most technology companies, for example, lose money in their first years as they make their investments in their technology and buy into or make their market. But in ten or fifteen years, if they last that long, they will be generating significant cash and thus value for their shareholders. That is the gamble you take as an investor. The phrase 'if they last that long' is a very important one, because many don't. But some do become near monopolies and generate massive amounts of money.

It is why, when I am looking at investments, especially in Tech companies, I look at the team and the vision, the people inventing and running the business. I want to know, understand and be able to buy into a shared vision with them and see how they are going to grow and last.

What sets some companies apart from others?
I think most examples of high growth companies I have seen and liked, and sometimes been smart enough to invest in, identified a niche they could exploit first, and they also had something special. Something nobody else had, or it would take time for competitors to duplicate or catch up to. Sometimes it was a specific technology, like my old company Trade Extensions' optimisation algorithms, or it was a clever vision of where they could deploy their technology, and a plan to make it happen.

A good example of this is PayPal, which is documented well in their co-founder Peter Thiel's book, *Zero to One*. Their first smart move was to set their sights on eBay auction users. They saw that eBay had a few thousand high-volume power sellers and it took them only three months to secure 25% of these as PayPal users. It was a smart play that cost them far less than trying to search for these users in a morass of potential smaller users. It was a clear business play that paid dividends and helped them start to scale.

Another example I like is Amazon. People said they disrupted the retail book industry, but I don't think they did. They didn't invent something new, they simply changed the way the market worked. They placed orders on publishers when somebody bought a book on their website and then sent it to the consumer. In a famous legal case, Barnes & Nobel, the book retailer, even tried to label Amazon a 'book broker', not a retailer.

Amazon saw that books were easy to ship to people's homes and, by building a logistics network around this fact, they were soon able to scale to include DVDs and CDs to their growing portfolio. Sales grew into pretty much every area of our lives. Then, because of this massive growth, they got very good at web hosting and services and Amazon Web Services was born.

So yes, there are some massively successful companies that go all out for growth and capitalise on 'first mover advantage', gaining a dominant or even a monopolistic market position. But, as Peter Thiel states in his book, he feels it is better to be the last mover.

He discounts received wisdom and counters the idea of 'first mover advantage' by stating that the only real game in town is generating significant cash flow in the future. He postulates that last movers, the people who make the last great developments in a specific market, are the ones who really enjoy years, or decades, of monopoly profits. They do this by dominating a small niche and scaling from there, often by unseating the first mover.

So, if you are not the first mover in the market, it is not a disaster. Business is a long game that needs strategy and vision. If you can see a way to unseat a first mover, and you can scale it, you may be the one who wins the race in the end. Personally, I prefer to invest in those companies, but it depends upon your risk appetite. There is no right answer.

CHAPTER 2 – ON MARKETING

Marketing has a single simple purpose in my view. It is the things you do that create awareness of what you are offering, and it starts to get your potential customers and clients on the path to buying what you are offering.

In this chapter I will share with you some of the things you should do and some of the things you should really avoid. I will cover how you can engineer free publicity and encourage you to get your marketing right, trying not to waste your money.

People are out there whose business is to sell you marketing services. It is easy to be seduced with the ideas and concepts. But remember one thing above all. They will be working for you and are there to help you reach your potential customers and retain and upsell to your existing ones. If they don't treat you as a sophisticated consumer of their services, find an agency or person who does. I say this because consumers are becoming smarter, they are more sensitive to what you do, and they work out your approach. You can read more about this as you slip into this chapter.

How to market your start-up

I, like many others, have wasted money in marketing the two 'start-ups' that I was CEO of.

Hindsight is a perfect science of course, and I can tell you exactly how I did it, and how much money I wasted... and if you believe that, then I suggest you don't listen to any major agency pitches for your start-up, you could be convinced you need to spend a lot of money. I am also not saying that you should avoid using an agency, some of them are very good. What I will share with you here is what I found worked whilst marketing start-ups.

So, if your selected agency doesn't talk about the things I speak about here then I would suggest you keep looking or do some of this yourself. Remember though, your time is valuable to your business. Rule one for me, and it's what I tell people who start up any business, is that you as the owner/idea creator should only spend your time doing things that add value to your business. If you write software, for example, the odds are you are not going to be the best blogger or marketer in the world. Don't be afraid to buy services, just make sure you buy the best you can afford.

Anyway, what should you be doing to market your start-up?

Well first, you do have to market, and it will generally cost you money. It will probably cost you more than you would like. As a rule of thumb, once you are two years or more into your business, I would say that if you are selling to consumers, you will probably spend about 25 per cent of your revenues on marketing. If you are selling to businesses, then somewhere between 5 and 10 per cent is more the norm. Remember though, your early marketing is simply to make your potential clients know you are there and to prove your right to be there, that you are going to add value to their lives. People can only buy from you if they have heard of you.

First you need a website. Simply building a cool website and hoping for the best is not enough though.

Most people now look for the goods or services they want via the web in the first instance. What I mean by a good website is not something you spend hours coding in HTML, use one of the companies that allow you to build, and most importantly regularly change, your company website. Most of these companies have excellent templates for you to use and, in addition, many of them have a whole host of individuals who have built and sell additional templates, so that with a little judicious searching you can find something that you can make unique and attractive. Have some fun and google 'award-winning websites' before you start to build yours. I am not suggesting you copy what you find there, but you will find examples of what works for other people, resonates with your potential clients and makes your website look cool and modern. Something else I suggest you avoid is people who tell you they will 'do search engine optimisation' for you. If your website is relevant, contains the keywords that are relevant to your product or service and has regular content changes, you will find yourself climbing the search engine rankings without having to spend a penny. I can hear the objectors now, but trust me, what I say works. Especially when you combine your website with digital marketing. The other truth about this is that, by the time you read this, Google will once again have changed the way that they rank websites and search engine optimisation may be required. It's a changing world we live and work in!

Next, you really do need to blog about your industry. Note I don't say blog about your product or service.

Your blog should be almost company neutral. You want to be seen as an expert in your field, not somebody who writes advertising copy for your own product. Consumers are very sophisticated, and they see through thinly veiled blogs and articles that just push a product. LinkedIn is full of these, for example, and they are boring. Write about your passions and what you know of your industry. Share insights and data, share your knowledge, and ensure your blog adds some value to the people who read it. Also, be prepared to enter conversations with your readers. Note I say conversations and not arguments. You want to be seen as the industry guru who is also willing to learn. When you are seen this way then people will come to trust the goods and services your company provides.

Whilst we are on the subject of blogs, seek out those good quality blogs written about your industry. Get to know the bloggers and offer them guest articles that are exclusive to them. They are often seeking excellent content. If you are in a B2B start-up, you can always 'like' or 'share' your posts on these blogs. If those bloggers are happy to link to your website in their articles, all the better. Look for opportunities to become sponsors on those blogs. After all this is where your potential clients are; there is rarely a better way to raise the awareness of your business.

Thirdly, develop and invest in a digital marketing plan with paid adverts. It can be much cheaper than you think and allows you to laser focus your adverts, information and offers. Be selective about how you spend your money and remember, most channels' providers in effect 'auction' the advertising space you are seeking using keywords and demographics. The more popular your keyword is the more it will cost you to appear in searches and feeds. If you are selling insurance, loans or mortgages then be prepared to be making major investments to get any impressions. If you are in the B2C sector then you need to be working with Google AdWords, Facebook and YouTube at the least. If you are in a B2B environment then LinkedIn and Google AdWords are essential, but I have also driven some very good results from investments in YouTube and Twitter, somewhat I admit, to my surprise.

Social media is one area which continues to evolve very quickly, and it is perhaps the one area where I would say use a specialist agency to manage the technical aspects of your campaigns. A great digital agency can make a huge difference not just to how much you spend but to the results you achieve. As in everything marketing, quality content is key. Make available good, interesting content. Things such as infographics, how-to guides, customer video testimonials and survey results all play very well.

If, after all of this, you have some money to spare then I would suggest you sponsor a local event or club. For example, if you are starting an online business selling bicycle parts then sponsor a local race, or better still sponsor a local cycling club, working with them to produce the best deal for both of your needs. Produce something which is memorable and sustainable, but at the same time make it clear that these things are not forever, although they may be. If there are national events that you can sponsor, then do that in preference.

Coverage and exposure are the key for your business at this stage and sponsorships can bring local and national media into the mix, allowing you a place to talk about not just why you are doing this but your industry and your business. The news media is always looking for experts in a specific field that they can call upon for comment when they need it.

You will notice that I have left email marketing until last. With the emphasis now on consumers opting in to receive marketing messages rather than 'cold calling' via emails, and the introduction of data protection regulations throughout the world, email marketing must become more sophisticated and permission based.

I am not a huge advocate of buying curated 'lists' or the services of agencies, few have been successful for me in my experience. Rather I would suggest you use all the above methods to build your own permission-based potential client lists. It is remarkable how quickly you can do this, and only then would I suggest you use email marketing. Even then do not simply send advertising via email. Remember, content and value are king. Provide value and something useful with every email and curate your lists. If people say they want to unsubscribe, do it straight away. A well-managed email list that allows you to take prospects on a path of discovery through to becoming your clients is an asset that you have paid a lot of money to obtain.

Finally, about managing your marketing data, the information you create with every marketing activity you undertake has great value. The one thing I would invest in early, in terms of software, is an appropriate system to manage all this data for you. Personally, I have found little to beat the industry leader as a product, but it is not cheap. But well maintained, accurate data will not only make sure that you can measure the effect of your marketing spend, but it will also do a great deal of the administration for you and help to keep you on the right side of your own data protection laws.

What I have shared is the fruits of my personal experiences. I am sure many marketers and agencies will either be supportive of or totally disagree with me. After all, that's part of the fun.

Feeding the marketing sausage machine

So, have we all been seduced by the idea that acquiring a potential client's contact information is the start of a successful journey yet? Furthermore, do we all believe that we can use an automated journey, using very clever software, to bring that client to the point where they are clicking on the 'buy now' button?

I can see some of you shaking your heads, some of you nodding and some of you wondering what I am talking about.

This section of the book came into my mind after a discussion I had with someone who, in the B2B world, was measured on the number of email leads they generated from their social media campaigns. They were wizards at building LinkedIn campaigns, they even got the best out of Facebook and Twitter advertising when they were measured on that one Key Performance Indicator (KPI). There was nobody better at generating leads, but those leads didn't appear to have a happy path through their business, they didn't close very much business from them. Much more of their closed business came from customer references, testimonials, and appearances at trade shows (prior to COVID-19 of course).

This doesn't mean that their paid-for advertising on YouTube, LinkedIn, Facebook and Twitter was a waste of time though. They were a start-up. They were educating the market; in fact, their product was so new they were building the market for it. The fact is, when you spoke to the people who bought their product at trade shows, or from cold calling, which they also did, then these people came to the trade show having heard of the company and the product. Their digital marketing was working, but it was not being attributed correctly.

At one point they decided to stop all digital marketing since its ROI appeared to be so poor. Six months later they found that their inbound enquiries, their trade stand visits and their sales growth had dropped.

Many of the email addresses they collected were personal email addresses, especially those they obtained from LinkedIn campaigns. A great number of the people providing their email addresses were students. One day the students would have the money and be in the right position to buy the products, but right now they were not what this company needed. On LinkedIn it's fair to say that most people I know use their personal email addresses, many are on there to look for their next job and are thus expecting their work email address to change!

Think of what this means as you collect an email

address from LinkedIn or most other social media. You put them into your sausage machine of marketing, sending them one (hopefully) useful piece of content after another, taking them on the path to knowing your product. What you are in fact doing is spamming their personal time, their personal mail that they read mostly when they are not thinking about work. I know it would annoy me, and I used to be a professional buyer. There are other ways to lead potential customers on that journey through your 'sales funnel' using other cleverer digital marketing techniques, and not just the ones that rely on cookies.

So, let me get back to my poor friend, who was being measured on how successful or otherwise she was, simply based on the number of email addresses her campaigns generated for her company's marketing machine to churn.

The way she did this was by offering great content to potential customers, and she would give it to them in exchange for their email address. We all know about the use of 'gated content' such as this. I truly hate it, and I confess I used to use that approach as well, until I got wise about the customers I was trying to attract.

The fact is they are sophisticated, they know what you are going to do, you are going to process them automatically. A day after I download anything in this way I expect to get a follow up email or phone call from someone who 'wants to help me'. I ask them often if they wouldn't mind coming round and cutting my lawn this coming weekend. That's what would really HELP me.

I am a massive believer now in the fact that, if you

have great content, it is in your interest to share it freely. To give it away, to make yourself look smart, to be seen as the knowledge leader, to be the company that adds value to prospective customers' working lives even when they don't buy from you. It's obvious, isn't it? The people getting this value from you will talk about you to their peers. They will come to value what you do. They will recognise you as experts and when they need you, THEY WILL FIND YOU.

At that point they will be ringing you or emailing you ready to buy. You will have convinced them without all those follow up calls you waste on the merely curious. You will have a relationship already with them. Their wallet is open!

There is research to back this up as well. Most people now spend most of their time in B2B buying doing research without even calling the supplier first. So why hide your best content behind a gate? They want to read it, listen to it, or watch it, let them do it in their own time, you will gain the benefit.

Incidentally, what about my friend? Well, she left that company and set up as an independent consultant to businesses starting out on their journey. She builds digital marketing and content creation strategies for start-ups and introduces them to marketing agencies that can help them act on her plans. She never uses gated content and she rarely fails to achieve her objectives; she has more work than she needs, and nobody asks her anymore how many Google email addresses her work was able to collect today.

Marketing at exhibitions and shows

At some point, if you are a start-up, or in the early growth phase of your business, you will get someone on LinkedIn, or a phone call, or a piece of direct mail, trying to sell you something they will tell you that you cannot do without. A space at the exhibition or show they are running.

Either that or you will have been proactive and decided that exhibitions may be a way you would like to publicise your business.

Well stop. Before you agree to a thing ask yourself a few questions and ask a lot of questions to the organisers of the exhibition.

What I am going to share with you are my experiences of exhibitions, both business to business and business to consumer. In my career I have committed my businesses to many of them, and I have turned a lot of them down. I want to take you back to basics to help you decide if a particular exhibition is for you and is it the right time to do it.

First, ask yourself the following:

- Will you meet prospects there that you would never have the chance to reach anywhere else, or in any other way?
- Can the organisers truly convince you that these prospects, or at least these types of prospects, will be at the show. Do they have a record of attendance that you can see and even verify?
- Can you secure a good position on the show floor?
- Do you and your people have the time to prepare and attend the show. Here you need to be honest

about the time it will take and, of course, the money it will consume.

- Do you have a relationship with a designer already that will help you design and build your presence at the show? I mean stands, boards, literature, 'giveaways', maybe a competition to attract the prospects you want to your stand.
- Are your current marketing materials suitable for the show, or will you have to, or want to, produce specific materials?
- Do you have the resources inside your business to effectively curate and follow up enquiries for your goods and services soon after the show without disturbing current activities too much?

If these tests are passed, then move on to other considerations:

- Are there seminar opportunities, round tables or speaking slots at a conference at which you can speak about your industry to show your thought/ knowledge leadership within your industry? Unless you are a prospect, an academic, or a personality, you are likely to be charged by the organisers for a slot such as this. You must measure the cost against the impact. In my experience doing something like this at a show/event drives far more interest towards your show stand and it is worth seriously considering.
- Is there a show media office/rest area and are any media previews planned? Will the organisers be using live feeds on social media to publicise the show? Can

you showcase your company to the media via these channels and establish relationships with journalists, bloggers or influencers who will be attending?

- Can you increase your presence at the show by sponsoring specific areas that are perhaps complimentary to your business? For example, if you are an office design company can you be responsible and be recognised for designing any breakout areas or VIP delegate areas? If you supply the catering industry can your products be showcased in the food areas that are inevitably present at these shows? My advice is look for things the organisers have not thought of and will add prestige or value to their show. Sponsoring lanyards, the registration desk, or giving out bags in the delegate packs is kind of alright, but seek out things that showcase your products or services and allow delegates to see them in context or, better still, in operation.

- Are any of your current clients going to be there? If so, can you provide them with a quiet zone on your stand where you can meet with them? This has multiple benefits including saving you time and travel costs that you would normally incur when meeting them, and it will make your stand look busy and interesting to prospects. I found that many times my existing clients were happy to stay and act as verbal references to prospects. People use this time to meet their peers in the industry, or even their competitors.

- Will your competitors be there? I ask this not because of the negative connotations of this, that you feel you therefore need to be there simply to show that you are trading, but with the positive opportunity it will present to you: to see what they are doing and therefore do some of your own market research first-hand.

Now, if you are at this point deciding that you want to be part of this particular event then recognise that you are in a negotiation, where everything is negotiable, not just the price of your attendance.

For example, back in 1999, one of my connections was building his own exhibition business in a very sweet spot for the business I was running. We agreed that I would henceforth, for however long I wanted it, have a space on the trade show floor at no charge. In exchange for this I secured all the speakers for the seminar program he wanted to run at the same time as the show for the first two years. I had the connections who could present well and would attract people and, of course, I ensured that I retained one of the speaking slots for my company as well. He went on to sell his business to one of the major events companies a few years later and, by this time, I had been part of a merger deal between my company and another. This was a truly symbiotic piece of business that helped us both.

A similar major opportunity will probably not occur for you, but as I said earlier, look for mutually beneficial activities or options and work with the organisers to produce and deliver these. Not every negotiation involves cash changing hands and, most of all, when you are at shows or events make sure your business always presents itself in the best possible manner.

Marketing, a way to guarantee your coverage

Have you ever wished you could write your own editorial coverage in a trade journal or website of choice? Or perhaps wondered why your competitors seem to get better coverage than you? Have you ever tried to secure coverage in the media to support your presence at an exhibition or trade show, but wanted more than just a standard advert placement?

Well, this is where the advertorial comes into play.

In most countries of the world, when a seller writes an article, or an extended advert about themselves, the publication must indicate that this article is not written by them and is advertising a brand. They often do this with a header or footer on the page. You will have seen these in the trade journals, websites, or consumer publications that your potential clients, and you, read. If you don't read them start doing so by the way!

Advertorials, of course, cost money. It could be that the media company will help you by agreeing to a feature article or advertorial about your company if you spend enough advertising money with them already. The other alternative is a pure paid for advertorial in addition to any spend you already have with the media company.

Advertorials, of course, do not carry the full credibility of articles written by the staff of the media company. But they do guarantee you the presence and space that you are paying for, and can be placed, as I indicated, at just the right time for your business. You may want to time these to correspond to a trade show, or a new product launch, or as a disruptor towards your competitor's activity, which does happen, and could happen to you.

So guard against this as best you can when discussing dates and placements with the media company.

The trick is you have to write something compelling. Something that your readers and potential clients will be attracted to. You need to make it look appealing with high quality images. The publication in question can often help you do that as part of buying this advertorial space. I always advise clients to provide the images they want to use, and also to check that they have the rights to use these images in all of the territories or countries that the advertorial will be seen in. The best way to do this is to have the photographs taken for you by a professional and ensure that they are yours to use as you wish.

In terms of subject matter, I always found case studies and customer testimonials worked best. People like to read stories so, if you can, make your advertorial a story. Other subjects that work include news about new product launches or interesting research that you have conducted. But a warning here, make sure you are writing in a style that is for your reader, not for you. It is easy to get swept up in the euphoria of knowing that your words will be in the publication but remember that this advertorial is not a vanity piece. Always remember its sole purpose is to sell your product or services, so make it do that, preferably in a subtle way. Another good piece of advice is, at the same time as placing your advertorial, place some advertising in the same media as well so your company name, brand, logo and what you offer is reinforced.

The last thing I will share with you on this topic is how

to handle the cost of placement with the media company. It doesn't always have to be just your money that gets spent. Talk to your suppliers, see if they will place adverts in the same media at the same time. If they are willing to do so, an incentive for them might be to have their company mentioned in your advertorial as well. I saw this done expertly by a baby food company who had a new way of delivering their product to the consumer using a novel packaging design. The advertorial was written by the baby food company but paid for entirely by their packaging supplier. The message is to be creative, look for ways to minimise your costs whilst maximising your publicity and be engaging to your reader, they are, after all, your next client.

How to get free publicity

Yes, it is true, publicity can be close to free. Not in terms of effort though.

I have heard lots of people say to me, 'I just need something that will go viral.' Well, guess what, you know all those massively viral videos you see on media like YouTube and Facebook? They have almost certainly cost thousands, if not hundreds of thousands, to design, build and develop. It's just advertising after all, and they have had great agencies behind them. The fact is you probably are not going to just stumble on something that goes viral. So, think again, and I would say think about Public Relations (PR).

When I talk about PR I am, in this instance, talking about the printed media, either on or offline. The kind of stuff journalists write and build. Now, let me break a secret to you. Very often 'journalists' in trade publications don't write anything at all. I know some trade publications in the B2B world who employ no journalists tasked with researching, crafting, and building stories and articles. They simply take press releases and articles from businesses in the sector they operate in and 'cut and paste' them into their publications. They have people who are really good at graphic design and selling advertising space in their publications and on their websites. That is their business model.

I am not being critical here, but simply alerting you to the fact.

In some ways this can be an advantage to you. Remember, these people need to fill their publications, they need well written copy, and who better to provide it than you. Very often you can get your story or message into these publications without even advertising in them as well. But one point I would make is that you need to make sure your customer is one of the recipients of your message.

All publications produce what they call media packs for their advertisers. In it they share with you their readership size and their readership demographics. If it's a B2B publication they will talk about the job function and level of the people who subscribe to them, or who are members of their community. Did you ever wonder why they asked you all those things when you signed up? It's because they use that information to sell advertising space or event places.

Get the media packs before you decide to target your efforts on a publication. Don't waste your time if the readers are not your customers. It's obvious isn't it, but I have seen media lists in companies of all the people they send press releases to that are basically deserts!

There are, of course, some very good publications, they have real journalists, and these are paid to write and research. They want to find good and interesting stories that their readers will find useful or enjoy reading. I would suggest it is these people that you really want to target, but it is not as simple as wanting to do it.

There are some ways you can make it more likely that your story or message is picked up though. In my experience, stories are noticed by publications in several ways, and it's rarely from a press release, most journalists get hundreds of these, so you must truly stand out.

My advice to people using a press release approach is, even before you send them, make sure you are landing them on the right desk or email account. Take the time to connect with journalists who write about your sector or geography. Remember, their job is to find interesting things to write about, you can develop a symbiotic relationship with journalists. But always remember the best journalists do their research, they question, they don't simply take your word for something, so always be honest and make it clear in your dealings what is fact and what is your opinion, and never lie. You will be found out and exposed.

When it comes to writing your press release there are a few good rules to follow.

It should be brief, less than one page if you can do it. Make sure your story is always supported with good content and that it is engaging. Photographs and well-founded research are always valuable to journalists and helps present your story. What you want to do is grab attention or build on a story you have already started to tell the journalist. Provide your contact details for them to follow up directly with you, or your PR agency if you employ one.

In your writing, try and see the story or messages from the journalist's viewpoint. They are doing a job, they want to be well paid, respected for what they do and they are thinking of their career. Therefore, things that are new, interesting, funny, or even challenging, play well and pique a journalist's interest. Good advice is to try to make any press release appear as if it written with the journalist in mind, not you.

If you have confidence in the journalist and their publication, if the readership is your audience and you have checked this, then consider making the story an exclusive to them. If you do this, you need to be sure of what is 'in it' for you to do this. Will there be some follow up interviews perhaps, or will it lead to a feature in the publication that you could write, or at least write with the journalist? Be honest in your thinking with the journalist, this is, of course, a negotiation.

I can hear you thinking already. 'It may be free but how do I have the time to do that?' Or even, 'I can't write press releases.'

Recognising your own limitations is valuable. It is why many PR agencies exist. They are filled with people who know what journalists are looking for (they have often been staff or freelance journalists themselves). They are often specialists in your industry sector, have those valuable contacts in the media already and will help get your story told. They know how to craft press releases and features and can be massively valuable resources to help you publicise and grow your business.

In the meantime, my advice to you, if you are a start-up or in the early stages of your growth and you are struggling to get free coverage in the trade press, is don't get frustrated. I would suggest looking to place your story with local media first. They are often more accessible and if your stories have a local 'slant' they are keen to carry them. Keep your standards just as high, they have space to fill but appreciate well written content accompanied by excellent pictures just as much. You never know, a good local story can sometimes become a national or international one very quickly in these days of mass communication and the internet.

We have won an award!
Without a doubt in my mind, if your business wins awards for its work it is a very good thing. The publicity alone can propel your social presence to new heights and the credibility they bring with prospective clients can be significant.

One thing that is sometimes missed by award-winning companies is the reinforcement the awards give to those companies that were your early adopters. Those people who took the act of faith needed to trust that you would deliver against your promises. It allows them to reinforce, either publicly or inside their own organisations, or both, that their decision to use you was right. It shows that other people recognised this and that they had made the right decision to use you in the first place. When you win an award, remember to thank your clients. Those are the people that helped you make this happen and propelled you into the black-tied formal spotlight.

So, awards are great, right?

The truth is, like everything, only some are. Some are frankly garbage. It is not a popular statement I am making but it is true, I want to alert you to this fact.

When I ran Freight Traders and Trade Extensions we did enter award competitions, we actually won a few, and I am still very proud of that. The awards we won were all from very recognised bodies though, or the leading publications of the time. So yes, I still have the awards from The Freight Transport Association (now Logistics UK), The Chartered Institute of Logistics and Supply, The Wall Street Journal and a very special one we received from a client, Nutricia, which is now part of Danone, for being their supplier of the year.

We did enter others, but they were strictly curated. I had an approach with my head of Public Relations that we would only enter awards from well recognised, or leading bodies in our field. I strongly suggest that you do the same. Watch out for those awards that are meaningless trinkets, that mean nothing and are only put together to sell an event or advertising space.

I truly have lost count of the number of times I have seen the phrase 'award-winning' attached to a company only to look at their website and find out that the award is from a mailing list type publication that sells adverts and pastes press releases they are sent into their publication under false journalist names, since the fact is they don't employ anybody.

Be warned, these organisations still exist. I had one ring me this morning telling me that my Simplify to Succeed Substack publication had been shortlisted for an award of 'best new business publication'.

The thing is I hadn't entered this competition, I hadn't heard of the awarding body, I googled them as I was chatting to the nice guy who was telling me how good my writing was and found a website designed by a gifted five-year-old with none of the things that should be on a good company website.

I decided to have some fun and asked them how the process had been run. I was told about high-profile industry leaders on their judging panel, without any names being provided of course, extensive process, highly sought after, yada yada yada... I had some time, so I started to enjoy the conversation, and had decided to save some other poor person from having to listen to what was clearly rubbish. Eventually, when he thought he had me, I was presented with the real reason for the call.

Apparently, the winners were to be revealed at a gala dinner, taking place in London in early December and, as a shortlisted entrant (What? I told you I hadn't entered!), I could buy a table for myself and nine others, my readers, friends, advisors, contributors for only nine thousand pounds.

How honoured did I feel that I would get to sit and eat a probably very poor meal, with poor wine (but good company of course) at nine hundred pounds per head. In addition to this I would be allowed to display the winner's logo on my website and headed paper and receive a featured article, that I could write, that would be placed on their corporate website. Yes, that's right, the one I was looking at now, written by a gifted five-year-old. All this would be mine for a further three thousand pounds.

Funnily enough I declined the offer and told them to send me the award when they had decided the winner. I doubt I will see it.

So please, if you are entering awards make sure that they are ones that you, your clients and prospects will value if you win. Make sure that it is a recognised industry body, publication, or event with a recognised awarding panel that you can look up on LinkedIn at least. Check out previous winners and the history of the award. Perhaps even speak to previous winners.

By all means buy a table at the awards dinner, invite your clients along and make sure it's going to be good, don't waste your or your clients' time on badly organised, shoddy dinners that you will feel embarrassed about inviting people to. AND I would say NEVER pay to have your 'win' publicised. Good organisations do that for you because it is in their interests to be associated with good companies.

There are lots of joke, false, rubbish awards out there. Do not get dragged into the mire by associating yourself with them or, worse still, paying to be part of them. So many of them look like the résumés I used to get when we posted jobs online.

I lost count of the number of false degrees people

claimed they had from 'universities' who had sold the degree to them, sometimes including a full academic history of the individual's results. Some looked very professional. The one that made me laugh most of all was a website that is now sadly gone. It portrayed the University of Neasden, and the pictures on the website were of one of the Cambridge Colleges. Neasden is in fact close to where I was born, there is no university there, but there is a London Underground Tube station. I smiled as I googled a few more obscure Tube stations and, sure enough, the same images and words were displaying for Turnham Green and Perivale Universities.

Just like the poor, desperate people who had bought their degrees from these fraudsters, don't go and buy awards that mean nothing and will harm your image from equally unscrupulous people.

CHAPTER 3 – ON SALES

This is such a key part of a business becoming a success that it is probably the most discussed aspect of the board meetings I sit in. Plans are written and rarely achieved, and hours of discussions happen because of this in most businesses. People talk about sales pipelines, sales cycles, pricing, selling approaches, incentives, bonuses, and a myriad of other factors. They are all important, but the things people talk to me about most are things like the quality of their sales team, their ability to get a fair share of the benefits that they bring to a client or consumer, overcoming barriers clients drop in their way, often at the last minute, and the nirvana of all sales organisations: how to become a supplier of choice, so deeply embedded in your client's business that they would struggle to find an alternative to you and don't want to. All those things are covered here and the advice I give is proven to work, but it is not easy to deliver or achieve. If you find yourself nodding a lot during reading and thinking that you know all this, ask yourself the simple question, 'How can we do all of that better?' That is where the big prizes lie both in B2B and B2C sales.

It's only sales

I confess, I'm tired of listening to people who always tell me about how they can close more sales or help me close more sales. They tell me how sales is a science, which makes me roll my eyes. This is mainly because I'm an Applied Chemist by training and, along with Physics, Biology and Maths, those were the only SCIENCE course on offer at my school! I concluded that the sales training I was being offered was being branded as a science by their marketing departments because they felt it justified the price or was a point of difference between them and their millions of competitors.

Now, behavioural analysis may be a science, psychology may be one. Although I always smiled at the toilet tissue dispenser in one of the bathroom stalls at my university above which somebody had written, 'Psychology degrees – Please take one'.

Anyway, this is not designed to insult all non-scientists, it's about selling.

My training, after I gave up chemistry, was mainly about how to buy stuff. Both goods and services. I had a very good career as a buyer, and was told I was a very good one, before I went off into the world of systems and start-ups. Then suddenly, one day I found that I had to be a salesperson, and in truth I didn't think I would enjoy selling that much. I did a few training courses (some of which I finished, others I dumped), I read a lot of books and research papers and, in truth, at the end of it I became a good salesperson because I asked myself a simple question. 'What kind of salespeople did I like when I was a buyer?'

Note this was not asking 'what I would do if I was a salesperson?', it was helping me realise what I valued in salespeople. The fact is any salesperson must show the following three things to a prospect: They must show that they trust them, they value them and that they respect them. It's true from the other side as well, as a buyer you get the best out of salespeople when you demonstrate those things to them. It's just human behaviour, if any one of these is lacking in any relationship, I would suggest that the relationship is being built on quicksand.

So as a salesperson how do you demonstrate this to existing and potential clients?

Let's start with trust. Well, first tell the truth. If you get caught lying or even massaging truths, you will be found out and all your hard work previously done is gone. Next, always admit when you don't know something. This leads to the next essential. If you don't know something and say you will find out, do it. Deliver what you promise. Always follow up and make sure that you do the things you are meant to do as well. Something which can be overlooked at times in building trust is openness, share your thought processes and include others. Demonstrate that you trust others as part of this.

Now, how do you show someone you value them? Here things get interesting because although it is universal that you should say 'thank you', often there are other cultural differences that can undermine you. If you are working in different cultures, find out how to demonstrate that you value someone, or their work or effort. Do this by speaking to natives, get educated, understand how to address this issue on a local level. A good example of this is in gift giving. In some cultures, this is a matter of courtesy, custom and practice, in others it can be seen as insulting, or even embarrassing.

The rule in demonstrating that you value someone, or their work, apart from genuinely saying and meaning 'thank you' is that you take the time to find out what is appropriate. If you don't believe how sensitive this can be then try googling 'how to show someone you value them'. I did. Answer number five was 'be a hugger'. Answer number seven was 'brag in public'. Even in the UK that would make a few of us cringe with embarrassment.

Finally, demonstrate respect for others. This is much easier. I have always thought that rule number one here is to actively listen to people, check with them, make sure you understand what they are saying and affirm statements and thoughts with them. In showing this kind of respect you will also be doing one of the things all good salespeople do well. They listen more than they talk, they learn.

It is a great saying that people don't buy things and services, they rent outcomes. Think of the interaction between buyer and seller in that way and you will become a much better salesperson. In doing this, always also remember that you need to be polite, and you need to be kind in your dealings with prospects. This does not mean giving away the Crown Jewels, but it does mean offering things that are often of low cost to you but may be of high value to them. Finally, display patience, remember people buy to their timetable and not yours.

So, in truth, if you are just starting up and you have never formally sold a thing to anybody, these are some good points to stick to, they work. Even if you are a salesperson who has loved all the training they have been given, that's great, but please don't forget these basics, they really will increase your sales markedly if you embrace them and live by them.

Is value-based pricing the answer?

When consulting with companies about their growth, one of the topics I like to get on to quite quickly is value-based pricing. It appears to be everybody's eutopia, but it is also one of the most misunderstood in my experience.

It often surfaces in discussions with start-ups or early-stage growth companies because they feel that they are not getting the price that their product or service deserves.

The fact is many of these companies have already put themselves into a situation that will be hard to recover from quickly, in terms of pricing, because they have already set their pricing too low. This comes about for many reasons, but often it is because they have been desperate to sell something to anybody. They just must have the first sale, and it's the first sale that starts to cause the problems.

When I advise on and teach negotiating skills, I tell people the most important price in any relationship, especially for the seller, is the first one you settle on. This is the one that sets the benchmark, this is where all other pricing stems from. In a year's time, when you have realised that your pricing was too low, and the buyer is in front of you, what are you going to use as the basis for your new price? That's right, it's the price you charge now. I can hear a few of you talking about open and honest discussions, revealing situations, co-operative negotiations, and all the other ways you agree new pricing, but the fact is the first price that you settled on and have been charging is like a sword that hangs over your head, and it takes skill to remove it. This is one of the key reasons that I talk about value-based pricing, especially to start-ups who haven't yet made their first sale.

First, let me tell you what I think value-based pricing is.

It is the price your customers will pay for the differentiated worth of your goods or services when compared to your competitors, within a specific sector.

In B2C commerce it's the price people will pay for extra functionality or benefits. For example, an oven you can remotely control via an app, or a larger capacity freezer. It is often confused in B2B pricing for services as gaining a share of the financial benefits your services deliver to your client. That is 'gain share' not value-based pricing as far as I am concerned.

With this in mind, and especially if you are starting your business, it is well worth looking at value-based pricing to help you set your first sale price. Here is the way I suggest you do it.

Firstly, make sure you focus on the segment you are trading in. If you are selling a faster motorbike then you want to concentrate and focus your effort on those buyers who want faster motorbikes, not all motorbike riders, or even worse, all bike riders. This enables you to evaluate clearly how much your benefit is worth to your potential customer.

Next ask yourself 'what product would my potential clients buy if mine was not available?' If you can name the product or service, then this is the one that you use as your benchmark to set your own value-based price. Sadly, this means that if your product is brand new and has no competitors, value-based pricing is very difficult if not impossible to achieve.

Next, work out what sets you aside from this competitor. What are your key points of difference? In the case I used, it would simply be that your motorbike is faster.

Finally, you must find out just how much your potential clients would pay for your key point of difference. Often you can do this by market surveys, by talking to potential clients, by using panels. A word of warning with this though. You could find that different people place different value on your key differentiator. I discovered this when looking at a product that could be made truly environmentally friendly. I found out that females seemed to value this benefit more than males, and indeed that disposable income was in fact the biggest factor in people's willingness to pay extra for an environmentally friendly product. So do your research well and understand your true target market as part of your value-based pricing approach.

There are some words of caution I would like to share with you when setting value-based pricing.

Firstly, it could very well be the case that you have multiple points of difference from your competitors' goods or services. Do not take each in turn and analyse them in this way and then assume they are simply additive; they will not be. In the real world your multiple points of difference make for a different product or service, you must establish which of those truly add value to clients. I often see this in software companies where developers add function after function, only to find that clients hardly use those additional functions or don't value them. You need to either identify what is your true key differentiator and seek out its value, or recognise that you have multiple points of difference, all of which add some value to a customer, and then determine what that 'package' is worth.

Secondly, value-based pricing is based upon your competitors' pricing. If they have been stupid in their pricing and are clearly charging too low a price, then value-based pricing will not help you. Always, when you reach a conclusion about your value-based price, check it against the bare logic of your costs and margins. If you are still finding that you can't make money at your value-based price, you will have to determine why.

Value based pricing is not a panacea, it is a tool that you can use to set better pricing and make better pricing decisions. When done well it will provide you with clear reasons for your pricing, it will help your sales team's negotiations and it will help you maintain your position in your market.

Selling to sceptical buyers

In the early days of Trade Extensions, a company I was CEO for, I used to do a lot of the sales of the product. For those of you who don't know it, Trade Extensions was (and still is at the time of writing) the most advanced piece of software for optimising buying events. Buyers who used it could answer both simple questions and those that were far more complex. The software would basically tell buyers what their best buying solution was, considering millions of data items in making its recommendations. It revolutionised corporate buying and it was hard to find an event that it could not optimise, and this caused some real problems in selling it.

The problem was simply that, as the salesperson, talking to an audience of buyers I found myself answering multiple questions of the type, 'Well, can it do this?' or, 'Can it solve that?' with the answer, 'Yes it can.' I used to joke that if you asked me if it could make tea and deliver it to your desk I would say, 'Yes, it can do that as well, if we know the suppliers who provide that service.' Basically, it was hard not to create a massive amount of scepticism amongst the potential clients of the software when standing in front of them. Before any demonstrations of the software it simply sounded too good to be true, and remember I was selling buying software to BUYERS. It's not the audience you would ideally choose, these people do nothing else for a living except buy stuff.

Anyway, this isn't about how great a salesperson I was, trust me, there are many better than me. It's about how you deal with the sceptical buyer when you are trying to sell your goods or services. It's one of the things I get asked most often, and the solution is quite simple, but it must be handled in the right way.

We have all found ourselves talking to a sceptical buyer. I loved them because it invariably meant that they were engaged and interested in what I had for sale. It's not a negative buying signal, I see scepticism as a very positive signal. The phrases, 'you all say that', 'your claims are just the same as everybody else', 'I'm not convinced', 'I don't believe you', 'nothing can be that good', are all signs of scepticism. Those are just a few examples. What you as the salesperson must do is probe behind those statements and find a way to prove your claims to them. Let your potential client guide you, find out what is causing the sceptical response and address it. Learn to question and listen to the answers, don't just keep gushing on about your wonderful solution.

It is a fact that some buyers adopt a sceptical attitude to all salespeople. They enjoy being difficult to deal with. It is their mode of operation. It goes back to the long-held attitude that in a negotiation somebody must win, and somebody must lose. It's old fashioned I know, but it is also part of human nature, especially if the buyer is using make-believe scepticism to exert power in the negotiation or to try to establish authority. I would say all buyers do this at times, I know I did when I was a buyer. It is often used to create doubt about the sale and drive to a lower price. But, even if this is the reason for the scepticism, they are still engaged, still in conversation with you and giving you the opportunity to work with them to get to the conclusion that they should buy from you.

The way you overcome the true sceptical buyer starts long before the scepticism shows in your dealings. It starts with you demonstrating your professionalism and integrity from the first contact you make with the potential client. Your attitude about your product or the services you are selling must be one of belief in what you are doing and selling. It isn't about your salary and commission payment. The sale will be much easier for you when you are convinced that what you have for sale will be beneficial for the client. In the case of the software I was selling I knew that it would offer massive benefits to the client and their organisations, it came across when I spoke about the product. I was there to make their lives better, and yes, I benefitted too, but they got the biggest share of the benefits available.

Now, back to dealing with the sceptical buyer. The one who is narrowing their eyes and leaning back in their seat with their arms folded and saying, 'I don't believe you' or 'really?' with that higher pitch in their voice. The first thing to do is recognise that and echo it back to them, say, 'I'm clearly not convincing you of just how good this is, or what it can do for you.' Then start that probing I mentioned earlier. Find out exactly what is causing that reaction, it is more than likely to be one or two things you have said or shown and identifying them will let you choose the appropriate mechanism you have in your armoury to address those concerns.

Something which is very important in this process is making sure that having identified the concern you address it, and only it. I have seen great opportunities lost by salespeople who are so enthused about what they are selling and being able to dispel a particular concern that they create more by not knowing when to shut up and stop talking. The best thing to say after you have made your point, is simply to check if what you have done or shown has answered the question. I use a phrase when I am training salespeople: 'Be careful not to snatch defeat from the jaws of victory.'

Typically, the tools you use to answer the sceptic are demonstrating that either their fears are groundless or showing them that your claim is correct. It can often be addressed by a demonstration of functionality, or a free trial, sometimes it can be addressed by an academic paper or article presented by someone the buyer knows and trusts. The best proof is having to hand a reference client or two who would be willing to speak to them, especially useful are those who had themselves been sceptical.

Incidentally, I would always allow potential clients to speak to existing clients alone, they don't need your help other than to set the meeting up and you will gain nothing from trying to lead the conversation. Brief your reference client and facilitate the introduction, but then stand back and remember to follow up with both parties after they have spoken and say thank you. Also, never miss the opportunity to create a new reference client from the sceptical client. When you provide access to a reference client always ask if they in turn will be willing to be a reference client if they buy what you are selling and are happy with it. It's hard for them to say no at that point.

Reflect your prospect's needs

I spent a proportion of my career buying software, I also spent a considerable amount of my professional life selling it. I enjoyed selling it more.

There was one major reason for this bias and that was because of the number of poor salespeople I encountered when I was buying, and it wasn't just in the field of software. The most common problem I came across was the simple fact that often salespeople didn't listen and they didn't talk about my needs as a buyer. So, if you are involved in selling things or services to somebody, give yourself an advantage, learn to listen more than you speak.

I can see you all nodding as you read this. I can almost hear you thinking that you do that but let me test you a little. As a salesperson, when you get the chance to present to a prospect, do you find yourself doing any of these things?

- Using a standard PowerPoint sales presentation about your company and what you are selling as a means of introduction.
- Enthusing about the functions of your product or service, such that your commitment and excitement is clear to all.
- Running out of time to make all the points you wanted to make.
- Finding some of your audience must leave to get to other meetings or calls.
- Seeing your audience using their phones, tablets, or laptops during the presentation.

Some of these things are clear signals that you don't have your audience's full attention, some are warning signs to you that you may not be answering the real questions your audience has.

Let me address one point in that list that you may think doesn't belong there. The issue of your enthusiasm for your product or service. Many times I have stopped salespeople in their tracks when they start to get excited about their offering and use words like 'and it can', or 'it also does'. I really appreciate enthusiasm in a salesperson. I want them to believe in what they are selling, but I want them to keep it about me and my needs. If, for example, I was being sold the Microsoft Office suite, just PowerPoint, Word and Excel to make it easy, can you imagine anything worse than a salesperson trying to demonstrate all of the functionality? I use about 5 per cent of what those pieces of software offer me and when I need to stretch my use, I google how to do it.

Sadly, I have seen salespeople so often try and show me just how clever their offering is when it is something I would never use. I've even subtly stopped my own salespeople doing the same thing in prospect sales presentations.

It's like an exam, answer the questions you are being asked.

The real message of this piece is that you must, as a salesperson, be sure you are focussing on what is important to the prospect before you even start to talk. Do your homework, ask questions, read reports, find out what pain points the prospect has and address them. Selling is not about showing how smart or clever you are, it is about addressing prospects' needs in such a way that they will pay you to do it.

When presenting to a prospect do the following:

- Show you understand the problem or issue to be solved, or can explain the opportunity available in a clear manner the prospect can understand.
- Explain how your company's capabilities will help the prospect.
- Tell them what financial and resource commitments they will need to make for them to satisfy the problem or issue.
- Tell them how long it will take to reach the solution.
- Share with them what you and your company will do to deliver the success and what your strategy is to do that.
- Share with them success stories and contact details of satisfied clients that would be willing to talk to them for proof and reinforcement.

None of this is easy, it takes effort on the part of the salesperson and their team to deliver this. It takes research and time. If you don't do these things, if you use your standard sales presentation without tailoring it to the prospect's needs and issues, if you are not succinct and you don't show your prospect how buying your offering will meet their needs, then I am always tempted to accuse an organisation of being lazy. I don't want to give my business to lazy people.

My role as a buyer was to test the companies trying to sell to me to see what you could do for me and to create value for my company. I wanted to come out of each face-to-face meeting with a salesperson certain of that. I would always test that aspect of any sales call. I would re-state what my understanding was as the meeting was closing. The good meetings finished with the salesperson saying 'yes that is exactly right' and having to add nothing other than asking me, 'So what are the next steps to get your approval to purchase?'

Why didn't that negotiation work out?

We have all been there. We have walked away at times thinking, 'Well that negotiation didn't go the way I thought, or hoped it would.' Have you ever stopped to really wonder why.

The fact is you might have fallen into the trap I have seen a number of buyers and sellers make in their business lives, and it is a very simple one.

But before I discuss that, I want to take you back to your selling or buying training. Hopefully you will have had some and not just stumbled into your role ... many people still do.

In that training you will have probably been told, 'You have two ears and one mouth, use them in that ratio.' A simple reminder that the art of listening is one of your most valuable assets. Yes, I know I'm talking about listening again, but it is so very important. Remember it is perfectly acceptable at times to allow for silence in a conversation. Indeed, it can be one of your most powerful strategies, especially when dealing with those people who feel uncomfortable when the talking stops; they often start to fill the void with nuggets of information.

If you have done any advanced selling or buying training, you will have encountered the statement, 'In any communication remember the adage of the radio.

There is a transmitter and a receiver, both have to be working well for good communication.' Incidentally I would add to that. If a communication is found not to have worked, I would firstly question the 'transmitter'. I personally think the transmitter has the responsibility to check that the receiver has received and understood the message in the way the transmitter intended it.

Assuming these things have all worked, many things can still go wrong. One of the subtlest is people failing to recognise that when they listen to or read something their brains get the message through a series of filters. You may not be aware that you have these. They are filters you have developed through your life. They may come to you as part of your culture, they certainly come to you through your life experiences. Remember that your filters can trigger almost unconscious reactions in you that may make you like or dislike the person communicating with you, or like or dislike their ideas. Try and recognise what your filters are doing to the message and be aware of how they can influence you.

We are now moving to the real point I want to make, and it is a very simple one.

Have you ever asked the question of yourself, 'What would I do in their situation?' I would suggest to you that this is one of the worst questions you can ask yourself during any negotiation. It is irrelevant. The only question to ask yourself is, 'What will THEY do in THEIR situation?' You have to understand the actions, needs and motivations of the person you are selling to or buying from. If you allow yourself to be coloured or led by your own thoughts, emotions and needs and try and map those onto the person you are negotiating with, you can be sadly wrong.

This is the real reason why you should ask open questions, to learn the essential things you need to know about your opposite number's position, needs and wants. Try and make the conversations you have open ones and listen to the answers, more importantly perhaps listen to what is NOT said and then rephrase the question to tease out the information you need.

In my experience you are rarely negotiating with an adversary, you both are looking to achieve the same thing. A deal you can both walk away with feeling that you didn't get everything you wanted but you got the things that were important to you. Deals like that are sustainable.

BUT I would suggest you will never get to that if you continue to map your thoughts and feelings onto the person you are dealing with. They are simply not you. Don't expect them to behave like they are.

Some thoughts on sales approaches

When it comes to B2B sales approaches, I have seen two that are dominant.

In the USA, particularly in the software or services market, where there are lots of new 'growth' companies, selling is mostly high pressure. If you are a buyer negotiating with one of these companies expect to get besieged. It won't be unusual for you to get almost daily calls, from multiple individuals in the selling company. Some asking what else they can do to help you make your decision, some asking if there is anything else you need for you to sign the contract, some asking if there is any further proof you need in order for you to commit to their product. Why do they do this? It's simple, it appears to work. I would lay a sizeable bet that the fastest growing companies in B2B in the USA do exactly this and have teams of highly trained individuals who themselves are driven by their own objectives, and thus their pay cheques, to get every deal over the line.

The other type seems to be companies who have a very laid-back approach to sales. If you are the buyer negotiating with these companies, it's a different experience. They probably ring you once a week during the negotiation process to 'check in' with you, almost being deferential and seemingly afraid to apply any pressure at all in case you are like the 'snowflake in the sun' and simply slip through their fingers. Their sales teams probably are commissioned, they get their pay cheques from the signed contracts too. The buying approach progresses, or stumbles, at its own pace.

Which would you say is right? I asked a few buyers I know over the last two weeks. These were old established hands who have seen both approaches. The answer I got back was, 'I don't care, I am in charge of the pace of the deal, and it will progress at the pace that suits me and my company.' The feeling I got was that there is bravado taking place on both sides.

For example, if a salesperson you are working with rings you each week the deal is not signed and says, 'When we jointly did the evaluation of the benefits of our product/service to your company it was 250,000 USD per week, are you OK to let that go again for another week?' How do you, as the buyer, feel?

If they ring you every day and say, 'Today, by you not signing, we are jointly responsible for letting nearly 36,000 USD of benefits slip away from your business.' How do you feel now?

It's a compelling message, isn't it? It may not actually be a lot of money to your organisation (perhaps), but if, before you have even talked about price, the sales team have worked with you to identify a real dollar benefit value of using their product or service, it's surely hard to bat these approaches away. The fact is time is indeed money when talking about benefits.

I have seen and been part of conversations like these, where the buyer will defend their position by talking about their own time, effort and workload, countered rapidly by the salesperson suggesting new temporary hires, or ways of working that will free the time which is causing the roadblock to that crucial (to them) signature.

So which approach is right? The answer, I think, is neither of them if they are used in isolation.

If your sales team is taught or trained to act solely in one of these manners, then I think you are heading for problems as a business. In my opinion high pressure selling often leads to outcomes that are not sustainable. It often leads to poor deals that don't suit the client and, when it comes to upselling, replacing, or renewing, the buyer is prepared, and often is looking to redress what they see as an imbalanced agreement they felt forced into.

By the same token, the other approach, where no drive and pressure are applied to a potential client in a selling situation, can lead to deals becoming stuck and to pipelines becoming clogged with deals that are going nowhere but still consume business resources. At some point in time you must accept the deal has died, or better still drive it to a conclusion. After all, if the answer is no, you want to know this so you can move on to other, more promising, negotiations.

My advice to companies when they are setting up a sales team is to go against all perceived wisdom. I believe you can teach sales technique but it's hard to train what some people call emotional intelligence. The best salespeople I employed often had no sales training, they had been buyers, they had lived the pain and understood the issues the client who is there to buy your product has. After all, remember that people buy outcomes, they don't buy goods, things, or services, they are buying an outcome. Some would even say they are renting an outcome from you, since there is always someone else willing to sell them an improved outcome compared to the one you offer.

So, my idea of good sales training is nothing like the traditional methods.

I tell people to treat others the way they would like to be treated. I have already talked about being trusted, valued and respected. In the buyer/seller relationship this is essential. Don't be extreme in your sales approach, understand your potential client. Understand they have choices and work with them to the natural conclusion that they should buy from you. Adapt your approach during the negotiation, push hard at times and ask hard questions, but know when to back off a little and give the prospect time to think, to process and to evaluate. Give them what they need to do this and check that with direct questions regularly. Don't be afraid to ask questions like, 'Are you the person in your organisation solely responsible for making this decision?' They rarely are, by the way. I have seen many deals fail at the last hurdle or get long delays in completion because this situation was not clear.

Do not be scared to make statements like, 'I feel that you are not going to buy from us. If that is the case it's fine, but I would like to know so that I can move on to other prospects.' You will be amazed how many times statements like that, made at the appropriate time by a salesperson, will lead to deals moving through a difficult phase and then on to a successful completion. If indeed they say 'No we will not buy from you', take the time to find out why and make sure you question to the truth in these circumstances, you and your business will learn from it.

One other thing, which goes against all perceived wisdom, is that I disagree that salespeople should have a large part of their compensation package based solely on their sales results. Rather than this, I favour companywide bonus schemes that reward everybody in the company in the same manner. Salespeople don't work in isolation; they are part of the organisation. I believe firmly that you all succeed or fail together. I like bonus schemes to be clear and fair and easy to administer. You can still use individual results to judge and coach salespeople but give them a decent salary, where bonuses are just that, bonuses paid for shared achievements because everybody inside a business has a customer. Make your bonus schemes reflect that.

Consultative selling

It doesn't matter what you are selling, a service or a product, you first must find out who the final decision-maker inside a business is for the order you are seeking. But to do that you need to set the target for what you want to sell. Are you going to be happy selling your office cleaning service to your local branch, or do you want to be the selected supplier for all their branches in a particular geography, a country or maybe worldwide?

The odds are, as your ambition increases, you will find that you must move up an organisation until you get to make your offer and negotiate with the person who truly controls the purse strings. Even then, in a big corporation, you will probably find out that there is no one such individual and the buying decision, although appearing to be made by that individual, is more likely to be a collective one. Invariably you must convince several people inside the organisation to make that big sale.

So it would not be a bad idea to decide what kind of selling approach your business operates.

Maybe right now you are a transactional sales business. Typically characterised by being 'one of many', selling on price or slightly better features, using your salespeople's personal relationships with a single buyer in every client. You can have quite significant sales revenues or volumes still, but as a transactional selling business you are constantly under threat from one or more competitors. The churn of your salespeople tends to be high, but it is a business model that works for many organisations, and in some industries transactional selling is indeed the norm with buyers often talking about the 'good deals' they made. I don't discount or undervalue this type of business or sales approach, but most of the time people ask me how they can become 'stickier' with their clients. One way is moving your organisation to become a consultative seller.

Consultative selling companies are those who have reached the pinnacle of their profession in terms of sales relationships. Not only are their goods or services greatly valued, but their advice is also. We all know the great consulting companies of this world like Bain or McKinsey, they sell nothing other than their advice, knowledge and expertise. Very often they work on a specific project, produce a suggested solution, sometimes help to manage the implementation and then 'roll off' from the client until the next time the client needs assistance. The best consulting companies don't treat their clients that way though. They permeate the client organisation, creating connections at multiple levels inside a business and in various areas of the business. In this way they are permanently engaged within the client's organisation, working in different areas and constantly slipping into and out of various departments, geographies or projects. But how do you achieve this when you are not a management consulting company and you are selling a product or a service?

In my view it takes three things: time, a well-executed plan, and expertise in your field.

Time is a given, it is rare that a business becomes an overnight success in any client company.

Your expertise must be second to none, and better than your client's. Never underestimate the expertise the buyer inside your client has though. You must remember that they have access to a much broader knowledge base than you do, your competitors. They talk to them, they share information with them, and they are trying to be the consultative selling company to your client, or prospect, as well. Buyers are trained to learn and garner knowledge, to acquire skills and expertise from their suppliers and potential suppliers, and it is freely available.

So build your expertise but do it in two areas. Do your homework about your competitors and your market but do more than this. Find out about your prospect. Become expert in their business as well, understand their strategies and their opportunities, work harder than your competitors in this area and gain an advantage over them. In this way you will become exposed to opportunities inside your prospect's business. If you are successful and they become a client, continue doing this with very active account management. You will be entrenching yourself in your client's business and building entry barriers to your competitors.

Some of the best examples I have seen of consultative selling in action have come in the software and engineering sectors. These businesses approach prospects on multiple levels. They have teams of individuals who use freely available information from major prospects to create reports that explain how their offering will create value for the prospect, sometimes even to the point of predicting profit, cash and share price effects.

Their salespeople, at the same time, permeate multiple layers inside the business and, using the 'value' report generated by their colleagues, gain access to the highest level of management inside the prospect by talking and presenting strategically. Alongside these efforts, even before the sale is closed, an account management team is working with the prospect, showing them how it would feel to work with them and the value they could create throughout the business. They are not only selling the product or service, but all of these teams are also selling advice, consulting skills and explaining the value they can generate for the client. This is how multimillion-dollar deals are constructed.

So, when you are a start-up, or an early-stage growth company, how do you mimic this?

The answer is you can't, but you can be selective about the prospects you are targeting and be realistic. If your revenues are less than two million it is unlikely that you will be securing work from the massive multi-national businesses that sign multimillion-dollar contracts. If you do, it will come through filling a niche, or via personal contacts, and these types of deals can be lucrative and educational, but they can also be flimsy and based upon one or two individuals inside the client business.

My advice is initially sell to the SMEs in your target sector, prospect properly and target your efforts. Set your pricing to match their capability to pay you the fees you need to create a margin for your company and be prepared to negotiate. Define what your ideal client looks like, critically assess if your offering will match their needs and provide them with measurable benefits.

Rarely will they have seen the type of structured and planned approach I am describing here in sales campaigns, and this will be to your advantage. In simple terms you must be seen to be bigger than you are, and you need to 'punch above your weight'.

Becoming a trusted business adviser that leads to you selling consultatively is not easy and is not a rapid process.

Typically, a consultative selling relationship starts with you discovering and selling to a prospect's needs and addressing their pain points. During this time keep the discussion not about features or benefits of your offering but about the value you are providing to the prospect. When doing this well you will come to understand the prospect's business and markets better and will be able to discover and understand their strategy and vision.

When you have gained this knowledge and started to do business with the prospect you must, through account management and senior connections, transition your business into the position of a trusted adviser. This is where consultative selling is found. It is here that you become an integral part of the client's business. Working with them to develop new ideas for your business that benefit both parties. It may be a new series of functions in a software business, or a new product or engineering solution that adds value to your offering. Many times, clients and suppliers grow together and move from being SMEs and transition into significantly sized businesses.

Growing together and collaboratively is a driver of some great success. In many of the biggest businesses I have worked for, or with, there were key events in their history where a supplier and the company took decisive actions and made commitments to each other that triggered their growth. In my experience these rarely happened unless it was through consultative selling.

All of this when you are starting out does take planning. In outline I always advise start-ups and early-stage growth companies who are trying to grow and establish themselves to build individual sales plans for target prospects. You won't win them all, but this approach will give you a better chance than those competitors who adopt a more scattered approach. So, in summary:

- Define your ideal client.
- Identify them through prospecting and lead generation.
- Engage with the prospect, talking about their needs and pain points and deciding if you can offer them something of value. If you can then...
- Initially sell against these criteria, not on function but on value. Tailor your responses and offers solely to this. Use supporting presentations or documents that speak to only this.
- Over deliver to the client when they are engaged and committed but ensure that your hyper-care or 'white glove' treatment of the client is bounded by time or delivery. Have a scalable delivery mechanism in place which you can migrate them into whilst still over delivering against your promises.
- Now move to a strategic position, sharing your market knowledge and your plans for your business with the client openly, encourage them to do the same and look for further opportunities.

- Agree pilots or developments together which are of value to the client but are also of generic value to you and are not limited to the single client. These should be aimed at helping the client deliver their strategy, and sometimes you may even have to help the client derive or clarify their own strategy.
- Continue to move strategic initiatives you build together into your daily way of conducting business. Continue to look for new opportunities to improve and develop the business of your client. You will benefit from it in increased revenue and a broader business which improves your own offering and market position.

It is a fact that not all clients will end up in such profitable relationships with you. At any one time your sales and account management team(s) will be operating in different ways with prospects and established clients. You should always evaluate and re-evaluate the Lifetime Value to you of each client or prospect and treat them accordingly.

Why it's important to be a good loser

A common mistake I saw as a buyer was the way salespeople reacted to the news that they had either lost my business or had failed to win it. So many of them demonstrated the characteristics of being a 'bad loser'.

I have lost count of the number of times I heard phrases like 'Well I think you will regret that decision', 'They won't be able to do what they have said for the price they are charging', 'They have an awful reputation,

I don't understand why you have made that decision', or worse still 'I told our guys we would lose this unless they...'

Those types of statements, to me, show the signs of a poor salesperson. You may be thinking that way, but you should never say it to a buyer. Every time a seller did, I made a mental note not to do business with them in the future. At best it shows immaturity and a lack of emotional control, at worst it is telling me, the buyer, that you think my judgement is poor and that I am incapable of making good decisions.

The salespeople who I valued most in those circumstances were those who knew how to take the bad news, did it in a dignified manner and expertly managed me. I took no delight in telling long-established suppliers that they had lost my business, or indeed telling potential suppliers that, despite all their hard work in trying to win my business, they had been unsuccessful. I still to this day say that the sign of a skilled buyer in an organisation is one that can deliver this type of bad news and still retain a good relationship with the supplier and the salespeople of that supplier, such that they will want to stay connected and try to win future business.

So, if you are a salesperson who has just been delivered the bad news, that despite all your work you have not been successful, what should you do?

Well, first never moan or complain to the buyer about the decision. Never, as I once had done to me, try to use emotional blackmail. In that case a salesperson said to me, 'I'm going to get fired if I don't land this business.'

Frankly for that comment alone they deserved to be fired in my opinion. Never try to offer any form of inducement to try and change the decision, in fact bribery of this nature is criminal behaviour in many countries. Never 'bad-mouth' the competition, and, as I had stated earlier, never question the judgement of the buyer.

The salespeople who impressed me most were those who had done their homework. Those who, early in the selling process, had asked me how I was going to make my decision. They had discovered what the 'winning criteria' were that I was using.

Those are the people who, the minute they were told the bad news, started trying to win my business the very next time it was going to come up for consideration. Not trying to change my decision, but already preparing for the next time; they sought feedback and they listened to it.

The best salespeople probe the rationale for the decision. Was it price that lost you the business? Was it your product or service, did it not meet the desired standards or match the quality that was being expected? Was it the terms and conditions that you offered? Even ask if it was something, you, the salesperson, had done during the process that had caused the negative decision. Importantly, do not react to this, you may feel personally upset or maybe even insulted by this feedback, but remember it is the buyer's opinion, it may not be true in your view, but it is an impression you created, learn from it. The buyer may have thought you were too eager or too pushy, for example, but with another prospect this style may be just what they value. Even though this is a sale and purchase between businesses always remember that it is in fact a transaction between people.

So, find out the facts about why the business was lost and judge them, and your own and your company's performance, against the 'winner criteria' you had discovered during the process. By comparing your performance against these you will be able to dispassionately judge if the feedback you have received is both valid and fair.

Next, make sure you maintain the relationship. Just because a buyer didn't select you this time doesn't mean you will not be successful next time or that they think badly of you. Use the feedback you have received and take the time a few weeks later to let the buyer know what you and your company has now done differently because of that feedback.

Make sure that you keep your knowledge of the market and that company in the market. Take the time to read their annual reports, for example, they typically contain a wealth of information that you can use. If you see articles or information that you think will be of use to the buyer, make the effort to share them with her or him. In doing this you are providing value at no cost to the buyer.

Share changes to your product or the service you are offering with the buyer, and don't do this simply by throwing your latest press release at them using email. Take the time to call them, explain it, and then follow up with an email providing more detail.

Every time you do something like this is an opportunity to build your relationship, to find out how the supplier who won their business is performing against expectations and judge how happy the buyer was with their decision. It's this that will start to show you when it is time to revive the sales opportunity and perhaps offer something better for the buyer in the longer term.

If you do this well, you will learn about your competition. You will gain information about what is lacking in your or your competitors' products and thus be able to provide valuable product development information to your organisation. You will understand and see trends developing in your market. You will learn more about yourself and your style and learn to adapt this to suit the people you are selling to. You will discover ways to use your company resources better, you will sharpen your sales message and sales approach and will probably throw out your fifty-page standard company PowerPoint sales presentation!

Simply put you will win more business and become more valuable to your own organisation too. Not because of your greater sales alone but because you will be able to help direct the offering your company is making and will know your own markets better.

Too many times I saw salespeople work hard to try and get my business only to vanish for a couple of years from my sight and reappear because their company customer relationship management software had told them that the contract they had previously lost was now due for renewal. They often got the same result after repeating the effort. The salespeople who often won and then retained my business are those who were the good losers and saw the loss as a positive way to learn and become successful at the longer game.

I invented account management

Of course, I didn't. But I did discover it, back in 1989, when I became responsible inside a major UK food business for customer service.

When I took it over the team was better described as 'customer order taking' and had come to me (after some persuasion on my part) from the Finance function inside the business. At the same time, I took over responsibility for production planning of the factory. I was already responsible for the logistics function, so I had formed the genesis of a supply chain function before it became 'sexy'.

But this is about the importance of the Account Management function inside a business, especially a growing one, which we were.

I took over this 'customer service' function at a time when we had too many out-of-stock issues, our debtor days were too high, and the relationship between customer service and logistics was poor because failures in order entry and lack of stock caused us to have to short ship product or do redelivery calls on customers. My discovery of account management was, therefore, very timely.

We were serving the UK grocery market. At the time about 70 per cent of consumer spend was being made in the top five grocery retailers, and these retailers represented about 80 per cent of our total volume shipped. I figured that if I could fix the problems we were causing these top five customers, life would improve. We would do more 'right first-time deliveries' and thus reduce our cost to serve these customers. We would have less invoice queries and thus have shorter debtor days and we would get cash into our business faster. The first and most impactful decision made was to make one of each of the five 'customer service' staff working for me primarily responsible for each one of these big customers. To become the customer's account manager inside our business.

This account manager worked for us but was also measured on the feedback given by the staff of the customer on our performance. They were inside our business, but they were asked to perform as if they worked for their account. The best account managers I put in place did just that, whilst making balanced business decisions.

Suddenly, instead of simply taking telephone orders, they were helping customers balance their inventories. They were liaising with our logistics functions to pull forward and push back deliveries. They were helping with the availability of both regular stock and promotional items by giving real feedback and by making trade-offs with the customer. At the same time, they were working with the salesperson inside our business for 'their' account to create a coherent and focussed link between all the functions of our business that served our customer's needs. My next move was to have these account managers become responsible for invoicing and cash collection and, surprise, surprise, our debtor days radically reduced as well. This was an early manifestation of account management in my eyes, and one that delivered massive benefits. Even though at the time I didn't realise I had discovered an early version of this essential role inside any business.

So let me bring this up to date and share with you why I think having exceptional account managers inside your business is essential. It's especially true when you are past the early stages of being a start-up business and moving into your growth phase, or indeed even if you are seeking to grow a mature business.

The account manager is there to represent your customer inside your business but to do it in a way that is beneficial to both companies. That is essential. If they are biased either way the role starts to lose its value. They must be involved in the early part of the selling process, probably in the second or third meeting so they can understand what is being promised to the customer and can assure the customer that they will be cared for once the salesperson has moved on to their next prospect.

Once the sale is agreed and you start supplying the goods or services you do, they are there to make sure the promises made during the sale process are kept. And I mean the promises made by both sides, you and the customer. They make sure the deal runs to its terms and hopefully that you exceed customer expectations. But the account manager has another role as well. They need to understand the customer's business and to look for new opportunities to either increase the volume and value of what you sell to the account, or to seek ways to introduce new services or products to the customer. They are there to 'upsell'. A good account manager becomes a trusted adviser to the customer and a revenue generator for you.

For start-ups, account managers are your growth lifeblood. Think of the service you offered and delivered to your first customer. You were so close to them that you knew everything about them, you helped them, you nurtured every part of your business relationship. Then you added your second, third and fourth customers and you felt worried that you were letting your first customer down or didn't know them quite so well. It's for this reason that the fastest growing and most successful businesses employ account managers, or at least operate a function that feels like account management very early in their business growth. Account managers are the people who drive your success.

You may think this applies only to B2B companies, it doesn't. If you are selling to consumers account managers have a key role to play. I have seen great implementations of account management in B2C companies where the account manager is, in fact, a group of well-connected well-trained individuals who are specialists in a particular client type or persona, or they are culturally specific, or they are trained in a particular use of your product or service. Queries are routed through rapidly to these individuals either by a chat bot or a real person. It is still account management.

So, find the best ones, train them well, empower them to act for your company as if they were the owners, and reward them well for their efforts and achievements. If you don't, somebody else will.

CHAPTER 4 – ON BUILDING AND LEADING YOUR TEAM

As an entrepreneur or small or medium-sized business owner, you probably are an individual that has some degree of charisma, and you will almost certainly be able to tell a good story. If you didn't have these things, it is highly likely that you would not have been able to obtain funding for your business. People tend to do business with people either they like or who are like them. It's true of funding businesses too. So, unless you have bootstrapped your company using your own funds and reinvested the sales into your growth, you are fairly certain to be someone people like.

That is great advantage, but it only gets you part of the way to building a great team and becoming their leader. Because as the founder, that is the role you are assuming, and you need to do it well.

In this chapter I am going to share with you stories of the great leaders I have worked for and talk to you about what capabilities a great team must have when you build your business and then grow it. I'm going to share with you just what people who led me did to get me to work the long hours I did and make the increased effort they all got from me. These people did one other thing as well. They changed the culture of the division, department, or in one case the whole company, where I was working. They inspired me and I tried to emulate them in leading the businesses I did.

So, prepare to drop into the world of Cadbury Schweppes, Mars, NASA and the Thames Water Authority.

Building the dream team

One of the books I really enjoyed reading is called *The Boardroom Entrepreneur* by Mike Southon and Chris West. In it they give great advice about becoming an 'intrapreneur'. This is somebody inside a big business who gets the green light to build a new business inside it. Very much the role I found myself in in 1999 when working for Mars, Inc. and building one of the world's first online platforms for freight movements. We called it Freight Traders. Had the book been available before I built and developed the business, I am sure I would have done better. BUT one thing I did get right was building my founding team, and in *The Boardroom Entrepreneur* the authors describe what is needed.

Let me pick out the particularly salient points and wisdom Mike and Chris shared about the construction of the founding team of a new venture and add some of my own thoughts for you.

In my opinion it doesn't matter if you are building your new business inside a big corporate, or building a new start-up, bootstrapping it or using angel investment, the rules of what you need in your founding team are just the same.

The simple fact is most solo entrepreneurs fail. Now I know you are all going to have one example you can throw back at me that disproves this statement, but I would venture that this is because you rarely hear about the individuals who started their business, probably while still doing their 'day job', and failed, gave up, ran out of energy, or simply became bankrupt.

One benefit of trying to build a team around you to support your entrepreneurial endeavours is that you get your first exposure and test of your idea. After all, if you can't get other people to want to join you, to work with you and build your business together, to invest their time and sometimes their money, well I think you should be asking yourself the question, 'Is this really such a great idea?'

As Mike and Chris say in their book, often the first and most important person you attract to your venture is a 'foil'. A foil is often quieter than the entrepreneur, is more cerebral, they often like to stay in the background while the entrepreneur does 'the sell' but they often bring a lot of the intellectual property to the business. In my case I was lucky, my foil was one of the best management accountants I have ever met and worked with. Not only did he bring that skill to the business, but he also controlled my worst excesses, keeping the business on its path. A good foil will constructively challenge and guide. They are an essential element to any start-up in my opinion.

Sadly, even two people alone can rarely bring any business to market, they need other roles to be filled. In Mike and Chris's book they refer to the other team members of the founding team as 'cornerstones', and I can think of no better way of defining the role these individuals fill.

I agree with the book here. It is suggested that a good number for a founding team is five. It's the lowest odd number that allows for informed debate and dispute resolution, even if it's three to two at times.

Now, I like the foil in any business to bring to the team one of the four additional disciplines that are needed to drive any business. These are, as defined:

- Innovation
- Delivery
- Sales
- Finance

I am assuming in this that the entrepreneur is bringing vision and drive to the business, although of course they may also be bringing one of these other skill sets as well.

Cornerstones, as defined, combine professionalism with a sense of adventure. They must share your passion and sign into your vision as the entrepreneur.

Let's consider each of these skill sets.

The innovator. Well, they are the person who focuses on the need or the potential customer's pain points. They bring imagination and more than likely build the prototype or outline the first code in a software business. It's said they rarely finish things and enjoy working on the challenge, solving it in a way that is, put simply, innovative. They thrive on the idea, not on the final product.

The deliverer. That's the person who is the realist. They move slower than the innovator, but they know how to deliver things to the market that will work and scale. The innovator is often off onto the next great idea before their first one has been fully tested, manufactured, or deployed. The deliverer is often a perfectionist, they think of things like cost, constraints and resources.

The entrepreneur often fills one of these roles, most often in my experience the Innovator. If this is the case it leaves a space free in the team of five for another role, and this is where my view differs from that of the authors of the book. They postulate that the best approach, if this is the case, is to find a second deliverer who perhaps concentrates on a key area of delivery that suits their own specialism whilst leaving the other deliverer to work on a broader outlook.

Next is the sales cornerstone. This person is typically not the top salesperson from a corporate giant. Those people are often used to selling the product or service they are given, being supplied with massive sales support, fed curated leads through their systems, keeping themselves up to date with product releases and undergoing constant, valuable sales training. One day, you will need those types of salespeople, but not now.

What a sales cornerstone is, is someone who enjoys really talking to customers, who listens and feeds back curated ideas about the way your product or service can be improved. They are comfortable with being told 'no thanks' because they understand that as 'not now'. They seek ways to change the answer to 'yes now' by listening and applying product and market knowledge they learn. In truth I never employed the classic 'salesperson'. In Freight Traders we employed ex-freight buyers, or supply chain managers who could empathise with the potential clients. They had walked in their shoes. I knew we could train them to sell. What you want from a sales cornerstone is a salesperson who brings customer insight and knowledge back, whilst always remembering that their job is to help make collective decisions about the business, its product or services. The knowledge they bring back from customer interactions should support the growth plans and help the business to scale. They should challenge the deliverer and the innovator and be the customer voice inside the team. Incidentally, as I have said before, I would never have a sales cornerstone in my business that had a compensation scheme based on sales targets. It biases their decision making in my opinion.

The next cornerstone role is that of finance. Here I do agree with the authors. In a start-up your finance cornerstone needs to be very comfortable with a large degree of uncertainty, but with a rigorous approach to management accounting. They need to be comfortable with carrying out all the accounting functions inside the business and having no assistant to 'do the boring stuff'. They need to relish the idea of working with systems that are cheap and simple and getting the best from them. They need to be zealots about cash management and be ruthless about it. Finally, they need to have the necessary skills and attitude to make a massive contribution to the strategy of the business. A good finance cornerstone will, quite simply, be the difference between success and failure.

Now coming back to the 'spare space' in the founding team I hinted at if the entrepreneur themselves is the innovator. In the book, Mike and Chris suggested that no new business should employ a marketer. My copy of the book was published in 2005, long before the days of massive social media marketing. I have not checked for a new version of the book, so I apologise to the authors if they have revised their view of this in later editions.

For me, marketing of a company is now an essential role. So much so I would have a marketer cornerstone, but again, not in the traditional way of big company marketing executives. In a start-up the marketer not only has to know and be able to segment the market, but they also must be something of a product manager as well. Their role is not simply to create leads for the sales cornerstone, they have a role in promoting the company and its products. They need to set the tone and the culture of the business as well as do the day-to-day approval, or perhaps even the writing of copy. They need to help the business secure investment, to attract money and funds to enable it to thrive and scale, and social media in all its guises is a very effective way to do this. They will, of course, be responsible for the marketing plan, and the business, no matter how small, should have one. The marketer cornerstone is the person who derives and dictates the 'voice' of the product or service you offer.

There is another role that the founding team needs.

If you are building a new business inside an existing major one you need to have a sponsor. If you are an entrepreneur, you are not seeking a sponsor. But you will benefit from having a mentor. Both provide similar but different roles depending upon your starting position, but both have the capability to produce huge benefits for your fledgling enterprise.

The book, *The Boardroom Entrepreneur* by Mike Southon and Chris West is still available on Amazon. If you are kicking your heels inside a large corporation with an idea burning, then get a copy and start to change things.

How to get the best from your team

I had a boss when I worked in a food laboratory analysing raw ingredients and production samples that was a master in motivating his people. He went on to build and sell one of the biggest and most successful drinks companies in the world and I still speak to him today, even though I worked for him over forty years ago. He is a friend and, to this day, he really does not realise how well he motivated his people. It just came naturally to him.

Over the years, in conversations with him and by thinking back, I worked out what he did so well. In keeping with the title of this book it was simple, but it was several things and he was, before everything else, consistent.

I will share with you what his secrets were.

First, what he did was get to know me, he always spent some time during the week just to find out what was going on in my life. He went out of his way to find out what my interests were and what my motivations were and, because these change, he kept himself up to date on this. I found out he even kept a little book of notes to remind himself of these things.

He worked hard to stretch me but provided me with the support and training as he did it. He gave me more and more challenging tasks and was happy to relax the pressure when he felt that I was reaching the limit of my abilities. I was, after all, a new graduate chemist with lots of theoretical knowledge, practical university laboratory experience, but not experience in a working laboratory. I saw him doing this not just with me but with other technicians and I was wise enough to see when others were doing better or worse than me.

In a conversation with me after I had left the company for a much bigger role, he shared with me something else he was doing. He was getting me ready to leave his department. Ideally he wanted me to get a bigger job inside the business but recognised that sometimes he would lose great people. He celebrated both with equal joy.

He worked hard on giving me opportunities to use my strengths and helped me overcome my weaknesses. Sometimes he openly shared with me why I would not be considered for specific roles or activities because certain of my weaknesses would put the role beyond me at that time. He always coached me or gave me the opportunity to work with colleagues or peers who had the strengths I lacked. In this way I simply got better.

Something he also did was give me immediate recognition for good performance as well as that which I received at formal annual appraisals. He was equally quick to point out my failings or mistakes, but always in a constructive way and with suggestions of how I could improve. Never once when working for him was anything discussed at my annual appraisal that came as a surprise. He prided himself on that fact.

He was also very clever at publicising the good things his team had done inside the business to his peers and his superiors. In this way our whole team was seen as the elite team in what was a large laboratory complex. We were the ones who invented new processes or produced accurate results more rapidly. We were the efficient team that delivered on our promises and there was literally a queue of people who wanted to join us from within.

We were among the people who got the biggest rewards, he made sure this happened. Our pay and bonus awards were on average better, we were the ones considered to act as ambassadors for the technical functions of the company and got the simple perks companies often award to their best performers. We got promoted into bigger jobs more regularly. He told me that he always wanted to risk giving a little too much or doing things a little too early for his people rather than giving too little too late.

Something he did superbly well was delegate. He would give parts of his work to his people, always making sure they could cope and were well prepared. Most importantly of all it was not always the boring work, it was often the exciting, groundbreaking, more interesting work. He was always there to help, guide and step in when he felt I was struggling though. Again, in a conversation he pointed out to me that not only did that make me grow and get better, but it gave him more free time to manage his staff and to manage 'upwards' inside the business to get more for his department in terms of work, equipment and budgets.

He held regular department meetings. At least once a week we would all get together and stop doing laboratory work and talk about the business performance, new products and new initiatives. He sought out our views on our own department and fostered a culture of openness. He consulted with us on changes he was thinking of and was always happy to change his mind if the discussion showed that it was needed. He believed fundamentally in the concept of the power of collective insight and wisdom and used it. He knew that the person doing the job was often best placed to suggest how to do it better. But he was also willing to be the one to take public responsibility, the one who made the final decision and would explain why he had come to that conclusion. But we felt our views had always been heard. Clearly this made us more committed to manage our way through some difficult times. We knew that we would not be involved in all decisions that had to be made, but we felt we were involved in those that had the most impact on us. In my management roles I would often say to my people that my job was simply to provide them with the resources they needed to do the job to the best of their ability whilst keeping the shit off their heads.

As you can gather by now, he encouraged a culture of sharing, especially information. He knew that information and often rumour would get to his people via the grapevine. He also felt it was better if news, especially if it was bad, came directly from him and was delivered to all his team at the same time.

We were also encouraged to take an active role in the budget setting and control mechanisms of the budget within our department. We would agree amongst us what new equipment was needed and compromise was always the order of the day. This meant we were committed to the delivery and monitoring of our results within the budgetary constraints we had collectively set. I used this throughout my career with all the teams I led, from buyers in corporate businesses all the way through to my management team in those businesses I had the pleasure to run, and to some degree own. Information is not power to be guarded, it is enabling.

He always helped his team, if the case merited it, to resolve individual and collective problems we had with other parts of the organisation. Very much like my 'keeping the shit off their heads' metaphor I used earlier. My boss loved cricket. I still remember him telling me when we were 'going in to bat together'. It made you feel good to know he was by your side. We didn't win every fight, but we won most and knew very clearly why we didn't win those fights we lost.

Finally, he made me realise that he could do a lot to produce the right conditions for me to succeed, but that I equally well had a responsibility to approach my work with a positive attitude. Motivation is not, and never will be, one-sided.

I still speak to my old boss today, although he is largely retired and living between two regions of the world. He has diversified his business into food manufacturing, hotels and leisure resorts and has created a fortune for him and his family. He still tells me that it was all due to being able to pick and motivate great people and I'm still proud that I was one of those people. I tried in my career to always do the same thing as this man. I was nowhere near as good as him, but if you try and follow his principles with your people it will take you a long way towards his achievements.

Everybody is a leader

My best friend used to be a professional footballer (soccer player for those of you reading this on the other side of the Atlantic to me). He played in a team that won the old first division in England twice in quick succession. I've seen the medals and the photos, I was alive when it happened, I know he is not lying to me, and can check the facts. He then went on to have a very long career in the English Premier League.

That's the kind of statement you hear in a British pub close to 11pm in the evening when a group of guys are boasting. I'm not, but I'm sharing this with you because of a story he told me from his career, and it resonated with me and taught me a very good lesson in leadership.

My friend was a 'dead ball specialist'. In other words, if his team got free kicks near the opposition goal, or a penalty, he was the guy they called on to take them. In his whole career he missed only one penalty.

The story he told me was of a penalty he had to take in a high-pressure game. This game was a local derby, and it was a massive local derby. Beyond the chances of medals and win bonuses this was about pride and 'bragging rights' in the city he played for. Local derbies, involving two rival teams who are geographically close to each other, have huge meaning for the fans of the clubs competing in them. Think Arsenal versus Tottenham, Rangers versus Celtic, India versus Pakistan.

The game in question had been very hard-fought as always and, as the game came to its end with only a few minutes to play, it was still a draw. It was clear the next goal would decide the winners and my friend's side were awarded a penalty. It was his turn to be a hero or a villain.

As the penalty was awarded, bedlam broke out on the pitch. The opposition bustled into the referee complaining about the decision, players squared up to each other like it was an ice hockey game of old. The crowd of close to 40,000 people exploded into a crescendo of noise and millions of people watching on TV suddenly stopped talking and drinking and recognised the drama of what was going on in that stadium.

My friend did nothing other than pick up the ball and place it on the penalty spot. There was no debate as to who would take this hugely important penalty kick amongst his teammates. It was his job. It was one of the things he was paid for. Fighting and jostling was still taking place amongst the players and the match officials as he walked back, ready to take the kick. He simply did not get involved.

Feelings were running so high amongst the opposition players that one of them even ran towards the ball my friend had placed on the penalty spot and kicked it away into the crowd, to further cheers and boos from the supporters. The atmosphere was reaching fever pitch and my friend told me he had never experienced such a situation. The level of noise and venom being directed at my friend must have been unbearable, and he watched as the ball he had placed carefully had been smashed away into the crowd by an opposition player.

Then one of his teammates did something that my friend told me helped him in his preparation for this game-winning kick. His teammate simply said to the opposition player who had kicked the carefully placed ball away, 'You are wasting your time trying to put him off, he never misses.'

Within seconds a new ball was provided, and my friend scored the penalty which won the most hotly contested local derby in years for his team.

His teammate who made that open statement probably didn't make it to help my friend, he probably did it as a kind of childish reaction to the action of the player who kicked the ball from the penalty spot. Much as a boy in a playground would say 'my dad can beat your dad'. But think of what that casual action did.

At a time of high pressure, faced with a situation he had not exactly been in before, where he was openly being intimidated, my friend had the simple reinforcement of a trusted colleague in his ears. 'You are wasting your time trying to put him off, he never misses.' The power of that statement and the timing of it was all-important.

A few years earlier than this, I was told another story. I had the pleasure of speaking to Mike Brearley, a former Captain of the England cricket team. He told me a similar story, but this time it was about something he got very wrong.

In his club cricket career Mike captained the English county of Middlesex. He told me the story of how he intimidated and nearly ruined the career of one of their best young players without meaning to at all.

When on the pitch with this player, if that player made a mistake he would often and repeatedly show his frustration with this teammate by closing his eyes, throwing his head back and looking away. It's a simple gesture that we all do at times, maybe best described as an expression of disgust, it often happens without you realising it. The problem is his young teammate saw it. He looked up to Mike and sought his approval. Mike told me that his head gesture was simply one of frustration with the youngster, it was nothing to him and he spent a great deal of time trying to coach and help the player one to one on and off the pitch, but that gesture was still there.

It wasn't until this was pointed out to Mike by another teammate that he realised the impact he was having. He apologised to the youngster, explained what the gesture meant and never made it again. Unsurprisingly the youngster grew to fulfil his full potential and played for England, scoring many runs.

This piece is simply about reminding you that your smallest of actions in the workplace do not go unnoticed. If you are in a position of formal leadership, think what your words and gestures do to others. I always try and catch people doing something good and tell them, rather than catch them doing something which is less desirable as my 'go to' method of teaching or training. The latter doesn't work, the former does.

Try it for yourself, I guarantee you get better results. It doesn't mean you can't correct errors and mistakes your team make, but it does mean that your feedback will be accepted as much more constructive and considered.

If you are not a leader within your organisation according to the organisation chart, then I have another piece of advice for you. Act like you are. You will get greater respect from your colleagues and your own leaders. You will feel better about your daily life and your actions will spread to your colleagues. You will probably end up getting promoted for showing your leadership 'credentials'.

Leadership demonstrated

I am old enough to have seen the first manned missions to the moon by NASA and I have spent a lot of my time learning about the way both NASA and the companies that worked for NASA to create the Apollo spaceships operated. They all provide fascinating studies in every aspect of business. Various stories I have been told first-hand by the people involved have made for some great evenings.

This piece is about the building of the Lunar Excursion Module (LEM). This is the craft that was built by Grumman in New York and took the astronauts down to the lunar surface and, after their walks, returned them safely to the Command Module orbiting the Moon. Incidentally those of you who are fans of the film Apollo 13 will know it also performed well beyond its design limits in acting as a 'life raft' to help the astronauts return safely to Earth in a stricken spacecraft.

More specifically, I want to talk about leadership and how to lead teams, especially in a start-up environment. Grumman itself wasn't a start-up, but the LEM was a concept, nothing like it had ever been built before. It had to be invented from the ideas of engineers, with an immovable time deadline and to budget. After all, the entire Apollo program was tendered, and the rule was 'lowest bidder wins'. I doubt that this rule was strictly kept, and certainly the LEM build went over budget, but is this starting to sound familiar yet to those of you building your first business?

I would say this piece of engineering wouldn't have been the success it was without the guidance of the lead project engineer, a man called Tom Kelly. He led the team of about 7,000 people responsible for delivering the LEM. His management style and leadership became famed over the seven years it took to get the first LEM into space and tested in manned flight.

Tom was under massive pressure; the eyes of the nation were on his team and there is a famous incident where, at a critical moment in the testing, one leg of the LEM breaks. One single engineer had, weeks before, made the calculation mistake that caused this to happen. Tom showed real leadership in dealing with this catastrophic incident that clearly had large budget and timescale ramifications. The engineer in question reported the mistake the very next day after the test, having checked his calculations overnight, and he came to Tom expecting to lose his job at the very least.

Tom made it clear to the engineer in a meeting that the mistake was indeed bad, and that it would cause problems. But rather than firing the engineer he told him to go home and rest. They had all been working hugely extended hours for many weeks. Tom knew that the important thing was that his team could admit their mistakes and do it quickly. That mistakes would continue to be made and, although none of them were desirable, it was crucial to the project that people owned their actions and did not try and cover up their mistakes. With that simple gesture he cemented his team's mode of operation knowing that errors, although bad, if they were admitted to and effort made to avoid them in the future, would not be punished.

How many of us can say we consistently operate as managers in that way? How many of us have had managers who do? Personally, I have used Tom's approach several times in the businesses I have led and worked in. Equally there are many times I haven't and every time I let myself slip and give way to the emotion of the situation it has taken me many weeks if not years to re-establish the relationship I had with the individual.

There are many lessons to be learned as leaders. The incident of the broken LEM leg and how it was handled is the stuff of writing such as this. Remember that, no matter how much pressure you are under, people do not make mistakes deliberately unless they are truly trying to sabotage your and their fellow workers' efforts. A mistake, after all, is defined as 'an act or judgement that is misguided or wrong'.

You may have massive personal investment in a new business, or be under other pressures, but there is never a benefit in losing control as a leader. Good leaders catch people doing things well and tell them. They coach and guide. Poor leaders foster an atmosphere of distrust and blame shifting. I know which type of leader I would rather start a business with. Think of Tom Kelly the next time somebody messes up inside your business, and act in the way he would.

Do you know the difference between complicated and complex?

I got a great lesson in leadership when I was working in one of the smaller units in Mars, from the unit General Manager.

I was leading the supply chain function of the business and every day, with my team, I was solving complicated problems. Note here I say complicated, not complex, they are two very different things, and my General Manager knew the difference and helped me to understand this. When I did, life became so much easier.

This was back in 1987 and in truth I didn't see anything I considered to be well written on this subject until I read *It's Not Complicated* by Rick Nason. That was in 2017.

In his book, Nason explains the difference between a complicated problem and a complex one. Most people use these terms interchangeably, I used to and I was wrong to do so.

The fact is a complicated problem is one that is hard to solve but you can do it using rules, algorithms, systems and processes. This means that although the problem is indeed hard to solve, once you have done it you can repeat it. When you recognise another problem like it you can use some or all your work to solve the next problem too.

For example, building a jet liner is complicated. It involves multiple parts and multiple processes, but once these are assembled and the resources are available a 'recipe' is followed and, at the end of the week, a brand new jet liner rolls out of your production line, every week.

By comparison complex problems can be recognised because they involve many unknowns and too many interrelated factors to reduce them to a set of rules and processes. Using the previous and related example, creating a fully functioning airline, that customers love, is a complex problem that uses complicated machines, the jet liners.

Going back to my General Manager, he taught me the difference, and in doing so taught me how to recognise issues in the business that fell into each category. He taught me that complex problems truly require imagination, intuition and creativity, and this involves you using your full brain, not just the analytical piece which is good at maths and process. What this means is that by recognising the problem type you can adjust your approach and not waste time and effort.

In his book, Nason postulates that the way to address truly complex problems requires you to use a four-stage approach.

First you must recognise the nature of the problem, is it indeed complex or simply complicated? If it is complex, then the next three stages should be followed.

Moving on, you need to change your expectations. You need to be comfortable with the result being that you manage the problem, not solve it. This requires you to be comfortable with ambiguity. It doesn't mean that you don't plan. In fact you plan more, you build multiple scenarios and the value is in building the plans. They help you think rapidly when scenarios arise in your business life. None of the plans you have is likely to be right, but in the act of planning you are preparing yourself to manage the uncertainty.

Next you must accept the fact that your approach to managing the complex problem will require you to try, adapt and learn as you progress. This is where real leadership truly shines. My General Manager said to me, 'It's OK to fail as long as you learn by your failures and your plan made logical sense.' He meant it and he stood by me as I continually failed and adapted to the circumstances I found myself in.

The final and most important piece, as Nason explains it, is to develop a complexity mindset as an individual. To accept that complexity exists and that it needs to be dealt with differently. Accept the fact that with complex situations you, as a manager, will not know everything and you will not be able to control everything either.

What I discovered from my time working with him is that my General Manager had pulled together a management team, of which I was part, to run a complex business. It was made up of many complicated parts, but he taught us to relish and be comfortable in this complex environment. What he did right was manage complexity and create a vision that we all signed onto. He told the story of what was possible, and what was probable, and we could all repeat it to our own people.

He made it OK to try things and fail but learn from the mistakes. He surrounded himself by smart people and let them use their intellect and experience and their technical skills, but he made us use our skills to solve the right problems in the right way. When we came together as a team the business was growing very slowly, with old products, it was not profitable. Within three years of his plan and vision all those negative things about the business had been turned round and it was transformed.

He often quoted to me the words of Dwight D Eisenhower: 'Leadership is the art of getting someone else to do something you want done because he wants to do it.' In our case it wasn't just the vision he shared with us, it was creating a mindset and a skill set in us that unlocked the paralysis caused by confusing the complicated with the complex.

CHAPTER 5 – ON BUYING

I spent over twenty years as a buyer inside one of the most respected buying organisations in the world. The commercial division of Mars, Inc. During that time, I was involved in many ground-breaking aspects and new technologies Mars used to maintain their competitive edge in the field of buying. From the early days of vendor assurance, through to crop forecasting using satellite imagery and the development of advanced buying and analytics systems. Mars invests in their buyers and values their suppliers and the reason they do this is a great deal of money they derive from consumers who buy their products goes straight through the business and into the hands of their suppliers, and that is the way it should be.

If you don't retain huge profits, I am willing to bet that about 50–75 per cent of your sales revenue moves straight through your business into the bank accounts of your suppliers and you need to buy well. I often see start-ups and growth businesses buying badly. Buying is a skill set you can train, even if it is part of someone's job as it often is in small businesses. Realise that if you leave vast sums of money in the hands of gifted amateurs then you will get sub-optimal results. You really should change that; you will be surprised by the increased value a trained buyer or two can add to your business.

In this chapter I am not going to be able to train you to be a great buyer, but I will share with you, through stories and examples from my life, some of the things you need to consider when buying on behalf of your business. From making sure that you are buying the appropriate things, all the way through to becoming a Customer of Choice and how to manage your supplier relationships to get the most from them, all this is contained here.

So, what's wrong with the specification?

This comes from my experiences leading Freight Traders and Trade Extensions, a couple of market-leading software companies that provided online procurement solutions. It led me to working with many global multi-national companies on their buying events.

You may find some of the points I make resonate with you. Either way, if you are a buyer now, or aspire to be one, some of this may make you smile... or wince.

I want to talk about specifications. By specifications I mean the way that you describe the job, item, or service you are trying to buy. Common sense tells you that you must get these right or you will find yourself in internal and/or external disputes. Worse still, you may even find yourself in court.

By the way, about ending up in court. I always advise people to think to themselves 'if you are reaching for the contract, you have probably already lost the argument'. Always try and resolve disputes commercially and NEVER take an entrenched position. If you do, the 'highly paid help', as a lawyer friend of mine once described his profession, is waiting there to help, and bill you.

Anyway, in my experience, in a lot of multi-national companies, I have seen specifications that range from the simple and excellent to the complex and frankly useless.

In terms of the poorer specifications, these often come about for one of two reasons. Firstly, they have often been written by people who have never been trained to manage risk or evaluate the likelihood of a particular problem developing. Secondly, the people writing the specification have often never actually used the materials or services they are specifying. Or worse, they have never spoken to the people who do. You may shake your heads and say 'never', but it is sadly more common than you would think. Add to these buyers who do not question specifications that they are being asked to buy against, and the problem can rapidly get expensive.

I recall helping a business run a European freight tender and, in reading through their specifications, it stated that 'refrigerated equipment must be used at all times'. I questioned this and I got back my favourite answer, 'Well we have ALWAYS used refrigerated trucks.' When I asked what temperature the trucks should be set at I was told 'they should be chilled'. I then suggested we speak to the person who had written the specification to find out more. Of course, they had left the company about five years before, but in speaking to the R&D staff it was clear that the specification would be more accurate and useful if it said 'the product must be maintained below 18 degrees centigrade'. Suddenly, for most of Western Europe, during most of the year, refrigerated trucks were not required... and yes, we did check that the product could also be subject to freezing conditions with no harm being done to it, for those of you about to say, 'A temperature range would be even better.' My point being that specifications should be challenged by you, the buyer, simply to make sure that you are not over or under specifying what is required. History has a habit of repeating itself and watch out for that 'we have always done it that way' answer.

My second point, about specifications often being written by people who hadn't either done the job or used the materials, does happen of course. I am not saying that the person who writes the specification must have done this, but they really should check that custom and practice in their organisation is in line with the specification. Again, I have lost count of the number of times I have seen a specification not being followed with no apparent detriment to the business, but for every one of those I have also seen a specification being slightly abused and costing money or causing problems.

A good example of this comes from my time helping people run logistics tenders. One of the most common comments I heard from the carriers who were bidding on flows was 'well that's not what they do now'. On multiple occasions I saw specifications that said turnaround of trucks would be two hours from entering a site, only to find that in fact it was more common for it to be at least double that. Incumbent carriers would rightly ask if they should bid based on the specification rather than what they knew happened.

On a side note, and it is a very important one, if you are choosing an e-sourcing tool to run your tenders, even if you are a small business, make sure it can effectively handle the workflow associated with changes to specifications that happen once the tender is on the market for bidding. You need to make sure all bidders and potential bidders get the same information at the same time and record that they have seen it. I have never found a company who has not had the need for that functionality at least once.

These kinds of problems are not restricted to services though. Many times, I have seen the specifications for materials having either errors or room for errors to be made. I recall a tender for a powdered material that was to be delivered to a food factory. It seemed that the closure of the 25 kg sacks, which the material was to be delivered in from the current supplier, was difficult for the line operators to manage rapidly, so they had instigated their own procedure, using a hook to split the paper sacks. Following a tender, a new supplier of the material was awarded the contract. They used the same type of closure, and in fact had a lined paper sack as their standard for their product. When a hook was used to open these sacks, the liner could fragment and suddenly the line had a contamination problem. The powder inside the sacks was perfectly acceptable, but the specification simply said, 'delivered in 25 kg paper sacks'.

In summary, I always advise buyers when they are preparing a buying event, be it big or small, to pay particular attention to the specification and question it as if it was the first time they have seen it. Question it to see if it makes sense, question it to see if it works. Talk to the people who must work with it inside your organisation and talk to your current suppliers to see how it works for them, or indeed how it could possibly be improved.

Specifications are not something buyers should simply treat as a piece of mail to be forwarded to suppliers; they are opportunities to improve things. Many organisations do have departments who work hard at making specifications work for their businesses and they do a great job of it. Many, though, have specifications that have not be reviewed in months or years. Part of a buyer's job is to make sure that they bring their natural curiosity to the specifications inside their businesses and trap the problems before they manifest themselves during a buying exercise where, by definition, emotions can sometimes run high.

Becoming a Customer of Choice

In my time as a buyer, I saw a few times when 'power' switched from the buyer to the supplier. By 'power' I mean simply that there is an undersupply in the market and buying and securing the goods or services you want becomes harder because you face more competition.

What this means is that suppliers now have real choices to make – and one of these choices is who they will work with. For many buyers it comes as a new experience and some, who maybe were a little too aggressive in their negotiations when it was a buyers' market, find themselves facing the consequences of losing out to buyers who were more considered in their dealings and have taken their time to make themselves Customers of Choice.

As buyers, it may seem unnecessary to even consider

being a Customer of Choice because, as we all know, 'the customer is always right'. But clearly it is never that simple, and what I hope I can do for you is explain why being a Customer of Choice is important. I'm going to describe what I, and several companies I know and have dealt with, consider to be some of the best practices that will help you become a Customer of Choice.

First, the advice I would give you is that the most important aspect of starting this challenge is to find out just where you stand with your supplier.

As a buyer, you really do need to establish just how important you are to the supplier. Put yourself in their position and evaluate your relationship. But importantly, do it from their point of view – rather than asking yourself how you would feel in their position, you need to ask yourself how they feel in their position. Reversing your view in this way will give you more of an understanding of your supplier and an insight into how they are likely to behave.

Start by reviewing past dealings with them on both a factual and emotional level. Have your conversations focussed on reducing price, being the customer that gets best terms or speediest responses? Maybe you, as a customer, have made a few promises that have not been delivered? Do you find yourself disputing a high number of invoices? Do you pay invoices late? During review meetings, is the focus on the supplier's failings or lack of performance rather than the positive things you can do together to make the business relationship better?

Answering 'yes' to any of these questions is indicative of a relationship that is not working well or is one-sided. Now your task is to find out the answers to the questions that will allow you to establish exactly how your suppliers see you and your relationship with them. Often this is not as easy as it sounds since, after you established and agreed the initial deal, you probably do not see the details of the multiple interactions your supplier has with your company.

In these situations, you need some guidance, and a good source of advice will come from your suppliers themselves.

A straightforward way to do this is to take the RFI/RFP elements of your current sourcing process, turn it around to face your organisation and have your suppliers evaluate you against it. Instead of grilling them about their performance, ask them to evaluate yours. Listen to their answers and ensure you get to the bottom of any negative comments. Most importantly, you need to demonstrate that you and your organisation have the willingness and capability to change. Fundamentally we are all the same. We want to be trusted, valued and respected, and often the first step in this process is to take heed of another common saying: 'Listen with your mouth shut.'

It can be quite a sobering experience, if you do this research thoroughly, for you to realise your custom is not really wanted, or you are a difficult client. What this is likely to mean is that you will be replaced as soon as a viable alternative arrives.

So, having found out from your suppliers where you stand in their eyes, hopefully it was good news. But if they do not yet see you as a Customer of Choice, it's now time to start making changes.

One way to start is by becoming more transparent and sharing your business plans and your business challenges with your suppliers. Clearly you may need to make sure you have non-disclosure agreements (NDAs) in place, and with this protection you should feel free to openly discuss your business issues and opportunities. When suppliers have a fuller and more rounded understanding of your needs and motivation it is very likely that they will become far more innovative with their offers and will help you to benefit from their experience and industry best practices – after all one of the reasons why you decided to buy the goods or service from outside your own organisation in the first place was to gain this specialist expertise and market knowledge. If you don't use it, well, frankly it's a little dumb.

Good sourcing software tools can help you with this. Not only is distributing NDAs or any other kind of data – documents, video, audio, images – easily managed by these tools, but the better tools will enable suppliers to act more effectively with the information you provide and be creative when bidding for your business. The advanced tools allow suppliers to offer alternative solutions, not just volume discounts, but genuine alternative offers that may officially be outside of your published specifications but are perfect for your needs. Let your suppliers guide you and, thinking back to earlier, do remember that listening to your suppliers is key to becoming a Customer of Choice.

It may seem obvious to start and maintain all suppliers with an equal footing, but until recently, technological limitations and the administrative burden involved in handling bidding events meant suppliers were not always treated equally. Today there is no excuse not to treat suppliers equally and fairly. Sourcing technology makes it easy to share business information in an open and controlled manner. What does need to change to become a Customer of Choice is the buyers' mindset. You must demonstrate to your suppliers that you listen and you recognise their competency in providing solutions – often solutions you didn't know existed.

Now let's move on to the last and probably the most critical point.

People generally value honesty and clarity in all their dealings, interactions and communications. Honesty speaks for itself and I will not dwell on that topic here again. Simply put, if you lie in a negotiation, and many people do, or have done in the past, not only is it unethical but you will also be found out and lose trust. Instead, I will concentrate on clarity.

Clarity in your dealings with suppliers covers many areas but fundamentally it's about managing expectation so both parties know what to expect and what is expected of them. Part of this can be things like jointly producing concise, simple specifications or agreeing and recording action points from meetings. But it is more than these administrative aspects of a business relationship – it is about being clear about what is demanded of each party, then measuring and sharing these results with all those concerned who can have a role to play in creating an effective buyer/supplier relationship.

Some consider information as power rather than a resource to be used and shared. Dealings between a supplier and buyer at all levels should be clear and consistent. People recognise plans can change, but your supplier dealings and relationships should not. It's vital to strive for consistency and clarity in every touch point and build mechanisms into the relationship that allows individuals on both sides to question and raise concerns without fear of the loss of either face or business.

Again, modern software tools help this approach. Whether it is a sourcing tool or a full procure-to-pay suite. Both, when used effectively, can facilitate the sharing of concise and clear information.

This clarity could, for example, be providing bidders with individual feedback during a sourcing process or supplying the correct information to ensure invoices are paid on time and completely without queries. Attention to detail is the key to this, and there is no substitute for striving to get things right first time.

Providing feedback should not stop when you have allocated your business. As a buyer, you should always insist on providing high-quality feedback to those bidders who weren't successful. Your decisions should be clearly communicated and explained, no bidder has, to my knowledge, rejected the opportunity to gain valuable insights from a bidding process they have been involved in. There is no need to reveal the final price you pay but, as a buyer, you should be willing to clearly explain why somebody did not win your business. A supplier who has been treated fairly and respectfully and has gained some market insight is more likely to take part in your future sourcing events – when you may well find you are very grateful for their participation.

In summary, if you understand where you are positioned with your suppliers now, ensure that your dealings are clear and concise and you make yourself easy to do business with, you will be well on your way to becoming someone who is valued, trusted and respected by your suppliers. Or, as I would say, a Customer of Choice.

The secret all good buyers know

I like watching some television and one of my favourite shows is *The Apprentice*. You know it, the program where a bunch of wannabe entrepreneurs generally be mean to each other and try to destroy each other to improve their prospects of winning the prize of a major investment in their business idea or getting a job with the main judge of the competition. I laugh at the way many try to undermine each other in the tasks to shine brighter than the others when clearly the aim is to lead and get the best from everybody in your team and beat the opposition.

Anyway, I say I watch this show, I don't. I only watch two episodes in any series. One is the buying task episode where the competitors are sent off to buy a series of somewhat obscure articles. The second episode I watch is where the competitors must buy from a wholesaler and then sell what they have purchased onto the public. The twist being is that it takes place on one day and they can restock from the wholesaler using the money they have earned from sales. These are great episodes because they show people's skills in two areas of business that are essential, buying and selling.

This piece is about the buying side of a business and one specific aspect of it, planning your buying strategy. More precisely it's about something called your BATNA. If you know all about this don't waste your time reading further, go and make a drink, watch TV, or skip a few pages.

If you don't know what BATNA stands for, then read on.

The concept of a BATNA was developed by the Harvard Negotiation Project and featured in a book called *Getting to Yes* by Roger Fisher. The acronym stands for Best Alternative To a Negotiated Agreement. What it is, is your final or fallback position in any negotiation, and many people say they have these planned when they go into a negotiation as a buyer but then slide straight past them in a desperate attempt to get a deal. I have spoken to a lot of would-be entrepreneurs who find themselves having to buy things or services to support their new venture and they don't have firm BATNAs. That is frankly wrong and will lead you into all sorts of future problems. For example, remember that if you are entering into a long-term relationship with a supplier, the first price you settle on when you first start working together is where all other negotiations with that supplier start from. I have told you this before and it stands repeating. It is that important.

So let me give you an example of strong and weak BATNAs to make it clear.

If for example you are negotiating your second year's office lease and you say to your landlord 'I won't renew my lease unless you reduce my rent by 15 per cent', then your BATNA, if it is a strong one, had better be another office you can move into that is equally as good, that won't cause you any business disruption and has a total cost that is lower than your current arrangements.

A weak BATNA would typically be something like trying to negotiate a lower than quoted price on the last two tickets for Elton John's last ever live concert when there are three hundred people behind you in the queue for tickets clutching cash in their hands.

The real message is, most people go into negotiations with either a weak or no BATNA, and it is often true of new business founders. For them the view is often 'just get it done', especially if they are spending some nice Venture Capital company's money.

So don't do it. Go into every negotiation of importance with a well-thought-out strategy and a strong BATNA. Your BATNA is the key to the strength of your negotiating position and thus almost invariably influences the result of your negotiation.

In closing, I will give you a real example of a strong BATNA that worked.

I used to buy containerised ocean shipping for a major manufacturer and needed to move frozen meat from the USA into Europe. For years shipping rates had been declining to the point where the ocean shipping companies decided to use the power of their combined might to drive up prices and they did this through a legal cartel. Overnight I was being told that my prices would be increasing, sometimes by as much as 60 per cent. I needed a strong BATNA since I suspected

I would not 'win the argument' based on the massive volumes I shipped alone. I did not want to move from containerised shipping, or in fact the suppliers I had been using, but I could not afford to pay the massively increased freight rates.

My BATNA was to have my cargo loaded, on pallets, into the holds of dedicated refrigerated ships I would charter. It was a lot of work to do, and it changed my storage profile and needs because I needed to fill ships to make it economic on a total cost basis. But I knew all my costs, I did my research, and I knew I had a strong BATNA. I also decided to target my new ships on loading ports and routes that I knew certain members of the cartel would find hard to lose my cargo from. I was confident going into the negotiation. The shipping lines in question had a weak BATNA compared to mine, they thought I had no alternative, and they were wrong. The negotiation resulted in deadlock, and I chartered my ships and delivered my cargo at a slightly elevated total cost. Within a year the weaker members of the cartel were knocking on my door to win my cargo back, which they did.

The moral of the story is BATNAs are essential, and they are more than a simple fallback, they are the lines in the sand that trigger alternate action if they are crossed, and they are essential tools for the buyer to have in their armoury. Take a few minutes before every negotiation to find your BATNA and use it.

How e-sourcing and tendering taught me to be a better buyer

The first time you use e-sourcing in a competitive manner you may get some surprises. Some will be pleasant, some will be unpleasant, others will give you a few 'ah-ha' moments.

When I was a part of a team running the first major tenders for logistics flows in Mars, Inc., way back in the late 1980s, the tenders were done using spreadsheets and paper. You had the choice of more than one spreadsheet provider as well!

What I want to do is share some of those surprises and moments that taught me a great deal about buying.

The first of the surprises was finding out just how many full-vehicle movements we had across Europe, and how many people considered them to be their responsibility! The second was discovering that we didn't really know how many European full-vehicle movement flows we did have.

This wasn't because we were not very good, we were just fragmented without a central source of information. Pretty much every tender I then became involved with in my career, working with multiple other major companies, revealed the same thing. Very few companies know what they spend at a detailed level even today. That's why software exists and thrives to help you classify, categorise, and prepare your business spend in such a way that you can identify your opportunities and get them to the market. If existing or legacy ERP systems had friendly and comprehensive ways to get data on business spend in and out of them, I suspect the market for spend analysis and classification tools would not even be there. But it's a multi-million USD per year segment of the software industry, so it's clearly needed.

So, let's get back to the first tenders we ran. It was before the internet, so we would send out boxes, and I do mean BOXES of paper, with the details of the routes we were putting onto the market. One route per page, detailing every aspect of the flow and we would ask for offers to come back to us via fax using bid sheets in our defined format. We would then dutifully key these into our own specially built mainframe tender processing tool, that at the time was considered the industry leader. We even won awards for it!

How times have changed, but one thing has not changed. We asked for too much information and too much detail from our bidders. This is the next learning point for those of you about to launch your first e-sourcing events. Only ask your potential bidders for information you will use to make your awards and be brutal with yourself. If you are not going to use a data element to either pre-qualify bidders using an RFI or use it to decide if you will award business to a bidder, then do not collect it. Don't waste your bidders' and your time collecting 'nice to have' information. It's not nice to have, it's a waste of effort on both of your parts. If anything, the use of e-sourcing tools and the spreadsheet-like collecting of offers has made this aspect of e-sourcing more, not less, likely to happen. Stop it now, your bidders will thank you for it.

A very interesting aspect of the first tender we ran

was a commercial lesson I learned, and it was on two of the flows that I was responsible for buying. I had inherited the buying responsibility for these flows from the previous job holder, they were from the Benelux into the UK.

The current carriers were doing a fine job and for two years I had been engaged in some quite lengthy and tough annual negotiations with them. My task, as I saw it, was always to maintain or improve their service, whilst minimising their rate increases, and that's a clue to what happened in the tender when these flows were put onto the competitive market for the first time.

I received offers from credible alternate suppliers, who were doing other work for Mars in other geographies that were more than 30 per cent lower than I was paying, for a truly comparable service. After checking all the aspects of these 'new' carriers' services I told the current carriers they would be phased out of my business and asked them why they could allow themselves to be so deeply undercut by so many competitors. The answer I got back surprised me. 'What would you have thought of us if suddenly we had decreased our prices by 20 or 30 per cent having worked with you for six years? We decided we would risk losing the business and hoped that we would have a chance to match the other bidders' lower prices in a dialogue with you when the true market prices had been revealed to you in the tender.'

The latter was never going to happen. We had made it clear that all offers were final and binding and there would be no dialogue about price after bidding closed. This was our first tender and we wanted to make sure we could not be accused of simply using it to benchmark the market. The incumbent suppliers lost the business with us, and the new suppliers did an equally great job. I had done a bad job as a buyer, and I think the seller had done a bad job too. Two years later when I put these flows back on the market in another tender the previous incumbents got a share of the flows back. By then the flows were so large I was looking to split the award between at least two carriers to reduce my supply risk and the honesty we had shared with each other in the intervening time paid dividends for everybody.

These first e-sourcing events I helped run all those years ago taught me so many superb lessons, not least of which is that market pricing is the way to buy, ensuring that you are comparing like with like, or at the very least being transparent to your suppliers about what aspects of their offer you value most and why. It taught me that a well-defined tender, where you stick to the rules that you define and share at the start, is essential if you want to remain credible. I learnt that transparency in commercial dealings is paramount, as is the ethical treatment of suppliers.

Many suppliers loved the honest feedback we offered them. We did not share winning prices as absolutes with them, but we did indicate their pricing position in the market, so they would get something of value back from the bidding process even if they had not won the business.

One very important lesson I did learn though is that of course nobody really buys on price alone. In our personal and professional buying lives we all apply constraints and conditions to our decision making. As in everything it's all about value.

How to gain and maintain influence with suppliers

Many things have been written about how you sell to a business, or more truly to a collection of individuals inside a business. Now I want to talk about how you buy from a business in such a way that you do get the best deal and build a lasting relationship with the business itself. It applies of course to those suppliers that you rely upon. Those suppliers that truly bring something extra to your business which helps set you apart from your competition and gives you a competitive edge.

Many buyers still seem to think that they hold the power in a relationship, and I have seen many instances where buyers try and exert this perceived power or leverage. One piece of advice I give both buyers and salespeople is that they must leave their egos at the door when they are doing business. I don't believe in a golden rule that I was once told, the fact that you as a buyer have all the gold does not mean that you make all the rules. If you try to behave in that way you will invariably be treated in that way and you will miss out on opportunities.

I was fortunate. I have been both a professional buyer and a professional seller, few people get that opportunity to live, learn and observe both sides of a critical part of all businesses. The exchange of goods or services for money.

Most good buyers can very quickly 'smell' something which is going to be critical to them or their business.

Something that presents a great opportunity for both and will make a step change in your own business. It may be a new product or service, it may be an opportunity for massive cost savings but, in some way, it is going to be 'game changing'.

When those opportunities come along it is time to start behaving like a great salesman behaves to a client. What you need to do as a buyer is begin to manage the sales process. Do not simply allow the agenda to be set by the salesperson, or their company, carry out all the things that are involved in the buying transaction such as checking for fit to your needs, evaluating the company you are buying from and all the other essential elements you manage as a buyer, but as you do this start to do other things as well as part of the process. Start to understand your current position and look for ways to cultivate the relationship with this new supplier.

To do this I suggest you need to get to understand three things about your new supplier. Get to know more than the salespeople inside the business, get to know the organisation itself and finally get to understand the strategy of the business and the people setting it. Simply put, you need the bigger picture; you need to invest in the supplier, not just with your cash.

So, when buying get to know the people first, get to understand their influence and involvement in the decision-making process. Never forget that they don't have to sell to you, but help them want to. Find out their reporting lines and start to discover other people within their organisation. Discover how much influence each person you meet in the supplier has and how they can bring this to bear. I would ask for organisation charts of key suppliers that I bought from or was likely to buy from. It helped me understand how they operated and gave me the opportunity to navigate my way through the organisation. It also shows engagement on your part and salespeople are trained to look for buying signals and engagement from the buyer.

Ask to speak to individuals. When I bought software, I wanted to meet the head of the people who would be supporting me. I wanted to meet and form a relationship with the head of the development team. When I bought transport services, I wanted to speak to the head of operations for the freight company and to meet some of their load planners. Every time I met somebody new inside a supplier or potential supplier, I was asking myself what is motivating them? Are they interested mostly in themselves and their careers or are they operating on a broader or higher level. Are they more concerned with the company image, its overall performance, or just that of their own area? Is their focus on the financial performance of the company? Finding out these things gave me both a sense of the company and the culture of it, but it also showed me how in the future I could influence it and gain advantage from it. With key suppliers I wanted to know how I could get things done that my competitors couldn't. Getting to know the individuals in the company, and their motivations, I found gave me significant advantages in the ongoing relationship.

If you document this work and formally build that picture of your supplier and the people that make it up, you will be able to identify gaps in your ability to influence. You will start to understand how decisions are made inside the supplier and you will begin to understand both the formal and informal processes inside that supplier's business. You will soon know who in the organisation you need to meet and form a relationship with in order to fill those influential gaps that you need to enable you to get the most from the supplier. You will also be able to establish continuity as you see people get promoted, move on and develop. Good salespeople will facilitate your discovery. The best will actively help you do this since they will be recognising what you are doing, the simply average will help you do this because it will be seen by them to be a significant buying signal on your part.

Doing this will answer the first two needs. Knowing more than just the salespeople inside an organisation and knowing the organisation itself. To truly create a path to influence the supplier you invariably need to go higher up the organisation and there is no better time to make the initial contacts at this level than when you are buying for the first time or seeking to expand your commitment to the supplier.

With key suppliers, or potential suppliers, I went out of my way to try and understand the bigger picture, to understand what their strategy was. To do this I made sure that I was at least introduced in the first instance to the CEO or a couple of the senior board members of the supplier. If they were a family business, then I wanted to meet at least one of the founders.

First meetings at this level may be nothing more than

a simple greeting if you are a relatively small client, but I always made sure that I was able to connect again in some way with the individual. Using LinkedIn or simply exchanging business cards always worked for me and always mentioning that you would 'like to understand more about the company strategy' was always greeted well. I always followed this up with the individuals and invariably I started to get a much deeper insight of what the aims and objectives of the supplier were, and I was often able to help them achieve this.

In this way I formed long-lasting relationships, some better than others, with the senior people in my key suppliers. I never overused those connections, I rarely if ever 'went around' my daily contacts in a supplier when I had problems, since doing this is almost always seen as a slight on your contacts and can easily ruin many years of relationship building, but I could have. This fact was known but unspoken.

The message is therefore a simple one. For key suppliers make the effort, get to know not just the people you are dealing with but the influential people who will be delivering for you and your organisation. Know how they operate, what motivates them and what they need, and try to deliver it. Truly get to understand the strategy of your supplier and if you can help them achieve it. In this way you will find your problems jump queues, your ideas and insights and needs are listened to and are almost always answered, and you will add value to both your own and your supplier's business.

A buyer's tale

Buying teaches you many things, one of which is what image does. I don't mean your own personal image, although this is vitally important of course. I'm talking more about the image your business creates, especially when you are buying from other businesses.

I got to visit and meet many companies in a twenty-five-year long buying career, and I got to see how good and bad they were at creating an image. Often the only impressions I had of companies before I reached their premises were their sales staff who had called on me, their company literature and their website. But let's talk about the motivations and observations of a buyer first.

As a buyer I was responsible at one point, either directly or indirectly, for spending close on 500 million USD of my company's money every year. But it didn't matter if that was just 500 USD a year. The fact is if I did it badly I would either have my career progression hampered, or worse still, get fired.

Think of the consequences of that for me compared, perhaps, to the consequences of buying something in my personal life, such as a new, bigger, ultra-modern TV to watch IPL cricket. In my case my wife would not be pleased, we have other things we could spend that money on more effectively, but we would find a quid pro quo, and I would probably be allowed to stay married. Is it any surprise, therefore, that buyers, when spending their company's money are far more cautious than they are with their own money? The risk of awful consequences is far higher if you get buying decisions wrong in your professional life. So when, as a professional buyer, I am approaching your premises for the first time, you need to think about your image. The truth is you only get one chance to make a first impression. It is an old saying, but it is truer today than ever before, especially (COVID-19 restrictions not considered) when we get to meet face to face again.

Let me give you a real-life example. A couple of years ago I had to sell the property of a relative who had died. It was an expensive property, and the proceeds were to go to a charity my relative had supported their whole life. I wanted to get the best deal in their memory but pay the right price for obtaining it.

In my experience, when people are searching for property in an area in the UK, they use both the internet and visit individual estate agents who specialise in the area. So I went to visit all of them on the local high street to decide who I would entrust with the sale. I was buying a service. There were five agents on that high street and, as I walked into each, I was greeted by the same scene. No defined reception area, no sign that my presence had even been acknowledged, an arrangement of desks with people sitting at them talking on phones or typing on computers, or worse eating lunch at them. People were holding conversations about money and offers clearly in view and earshot of other people and other clients, there was no privacy in any of them. This, by the way, is a common model for most estate agents in the UK, and in my opinion it's horrible.

None of them got my business, I ended up having a professional brochure created for the house and I contacted a local high-end auctioneer in the area who had a contact list of wealthy individuals. I ended up selling the property for more than any of the agents had valued it at and the auctioneer charged me about half the fees any of the agents had quoted. But the first impressions those agents created for me meant they lost what would have been an easy sale and would have earned them many thousands of pounds in fees for what would have been minimal effort.

Let me give you another example of how to get things wrong and right at the same time. I used to be a buyer for a company who believed fundamentally that the consumer was their boss, and that their job was to provide products that were of consistently high quality and provided value for money. One thing they did very well was drive value from their supplier relationships.

How do you think I felt when a trucking company in Italy invited me to meet them in their HQ for the first time? The building was a model of modernity and design. It was fully glass-fronted and looked like something a pharma company would have. As I walked into the reception I was confronted by not one but three marble fountains inside a cavernous atrium. The distance from the front door to the reception desk was a ten-minute walk. I would not have been surprised to find a food cart selling espresso with a seat halfway along the journey to reception so the weary traveller could rest. By the time I arrived at reception I was thinking, 'I cannot afford these guys.' I was right by the way. I am sure they could have done an excellent job for me, but they were specialists in carrying very high value goods where transport costs were less than half of 1 per cent of the sales value of the goods.

In truth the buyers of their clients would probably expect the glass and marble reception and probably did not care if they could have got the transport costs a few hundred euros per truck lower, but I did. Transport represented about 3 per cent of my goods sales value, I cared about less than one hundred euros per truck, because I moved a lot of them and when you are a high-volume business fifty euros per truck can quickly get to a large sum of money that could be better spent elsewhere in the business. The trucking company got the reception moderately right for the clients they were attracting, what they got wrong was thinking that I would be willing to pay the same to move my products as their clients were already paying to move luxury goods.

So, what really is the point of this piece? I can hear you saying this in your minds now, having got this far.

It is to make you consider the image of your business. In today's world it is very easy to be seduced into thinking that first impressions don't matter as much. They do. They matter even more.

Think about those shared office facilities that many people and almost all start-ups seem to use now. If you have visited them, think about the reception and waiting areas. Were you greeted well, was there even a human there? Was there someplace comfortable to sit and wait while the person you were meeting descended from fifty floors up in the sky? Did the premises truly represent the business you were visiting to do business with? Was it appropriate to your business and your budget? If you are thinking those things, well remember the buyers who are your lifeblood are thinking the same. They are evaluating you. It always amazes me that businesses still pay scant attention to their own reception areas and even more so to the reception staff they employ and motivate, lead and reward.

Sad to say your sales brochures probably end up in the bin, your salespeople are expected to present well when they come to the buyer's premises or meet you for the first time. As a buyer I expect that. What I like to see is how you live; what you think I would expect of you and how you present yourself to the outside world. What first impression do your premises and people create? An old buying friend of mine, who worked for one of the UK's major retailers, said to me once, 'I want to see where these guys tie their dogs up at night, if they look after them and if they feed them well, before I ever consider doing business with them.'

So just like you set your advertising to match your target audience, set your company image to do the same. If there is not balance in all aspects of your company persona buyers are trained to sniff it out, and that makes them start to ask questions. One of which is 'can I do business with these people?'

The devil is in the detail

I have met and worked with some of the best buyers in the world, at least in my opinion they were. I have also seen in operation some of the worst.

In most businesses, even those with dedicated buying teams, the buyers are often not the highest thought of individuals. But stop and think. For every hundred pounds, dollars etc. you get from your customers, you pass about thirty to sixty of those pounds or dollars etc. through your bank accounts to suppliers of goods and services. That is a lot of your money going out of your business, shouldn't you pay attention to it?

I continue to be amazed at how buying in many businesses is still seen as a poor relation to production, or marketing, or even finance. That may be down to the buyers themselves at times. Let me give you an example.

Many years back I was part of buying team who had a culture of reward and advancement almost entirely based on an individual buyer's ability to deliver savings when compared to the budgets they themselves had set at the start of the year. Yes, that's right, go back and read that again.

They got rewarded and promoted based upon beating the budgets they had set themselves. What do you think they did?

For me it all blew up in one buying meeting mid-year when I argued that I had done a better job for the business by coming in 'on budget' than all the other buyers who were now getting rounds of applause from their peers for delivering savings for the business. I was incredulous that the packaging buyer was now declaring that, despite reducing sales volumes, he was delivering savings of 25 per cent compared to budget.

Nobody asked him how much his budget had been increased by compared to the previous year. (It was 20 per cent by the way.) What made it worse was that because of this increase in packaging costs, thanks to his 'budget' (for what was a high-volume, low-price commodity product), we had to increase prices to the client. This left the door open for our competitors to undercut our prices. Is it any wonder the guy was buying against a 'reduced sales volume'. He had created the situation himself.

Now some of you will be saying that it's not the buyer's fault. The KPIs set and the rewards methods inside the business encouraged bad behaviour of this nature, and they did.

You will also now realise that this is not about buying alone, it is about looking at the detail inside your business. There is simply no substitute for keeping an eye on detail, to taste, smell and feel what is happening. If you are just starting up and you are going to be a success, you will do this naturally. If you are a CEO of a bigger business, you must do this.

Detail is everything and the best businesspeople I know are clear about this. They have their own ways to determine the health of their business. Some use dashboards, some use weekly cash flow analysis, client responses or sales, but they all have one thing in common. They all know what is going on and they have devised methods for measuring it. One old story I still refer to is that the founder of one of the UK's prime retailers used to walk their store floors on a Saturday morning with his wife and used to use the sound of cash registers opening, closing and ringing up sales as one of his measures of his business's health. If he could hold a conversation with his wife easily, he knew things were not going well.

This obsession with detail must go all the way down

your business, it must be part of your culture, part of your DNA. But there comes a warning with it, do not allow yourself to be paralysed by analysis. It has been proven that Pareto was about right. Most of the time good decisions can be made by good people with about 80 per cent of the ideal data or information they have available. This comes with experience, and if you are a start-up and lack it, then those are the roles you need to fill when you are starting out.

Coming back to my buying example, with my colleague who got a pay increase for driving up our prices and losing us market share.

How different it could have been if his budget had been scrutinised properly, had been challenged instead of just being added to the finance function's spreadsheets that spat out the answer at the end of the budgeting process. Or even better, if the company had a culture of excellence in buying, had trained their buyers better and really understood the key drivers inside their business by paying attention to the detail. The day the CEO of that business changed and a culture of attention to detail and rewards for the correct behaviour was instilled, was the day that did indeed transform them. They eventually became a highly profitable growing business once again. But by then I was long gone, so I missed saying 'I told you so'.

CHAPTER 6 – ON SCALING AND SURVIVING

This chapter is all about ensuring your business is here tomorrow and growing. Many start-ups fail within twelve months of starting, some stutter and bump along with little growth once they get to about two years old. I will be revealing why that is, and it may not be what you think.

I have also provided some advice not just about managing your cash, but what to do when you appear to be running out of it. Going back to shareholders or your bank is not always the best choice, and there are many things you can do inside your business to improve your cash position. I have listed many for you and used most of them at one time or another.

I can't resist a story and inside this chapter is one of truly poor customer service that I suspect, and later had confirmed to me, was caused by very poor attempts at scaling a business that was under considerable pressure thanks to a combination of a poor systems implementation and an extraordinarily successful new product and marketing campaign.

Finally, I talk a little about the view that massive growth rates are the sole measure by which companies should be judged.

Building a better mousetrap

This was inspired by a friend of mine, Mark Schenkius. Mark is now a professional trainer and lecturer in the field of procurement, negotiation, and sales. He is also the author of a great book, *The Other Side of Sales*. In it he reveals to salespeople how buyers think. I would certainly recommend it to anybody in B2B sales.

Anyway, Mark and I worked together at Mars, but this isn't about us buying stuff there, it's about building a client base when you first start a business.

The phrase 'Build a better mousetrap, and the world will beat a path to your door' is attributed to Ralph Waldo Emerson. But did you know that the US Patent Office has issued more patents for mousetraps than any other machine? So, what does this tell us? Well firstly, that lots of people have lots of time on their hands to think about inventing mousetraps, and that maybe some of those ideas were triggered by the Emerson phrase; and the people saw untold riches in their minds as they were designing a 'best ever' trap. Maybe it also illustrates how successful in evolutionary terms mice are.

The fact is pretty much every inventor dreams of and pictures their ideas leading to untold wealth and glory, or at the very least being recognised for improving the world in some way. They are also convinced that Emerson was right and all you must do is make the best or be the best and the wealth will follow. Sadly, that is often not the case.

Mark and I talked about selling B2B services the other day, and we both made the same comment. The fact is you really can be one of the best, and very excited about launching your new career, product, or service on the market, but invariably, soon after the launch, the reality hits you and the sales do not come flooding in. Instead, all those friends who promised to help you with connections, or sales, or work suddenly are not there anymore. I don't think that they are deliberately misleading you, often they are swept up in your enthusiasm for your idea, they truly want to help and tell you about connections they have, no matter how tenuous. Humans are social animals; we gain reward by being liked and one of the ways to be liked is to help others. Your friends are not being selfish, they are simply trying to be supportive, but in doing this they can lead you into blind alleys and cost you time and effort. You, as the business, must be strong for them and, just like an army medic in a battlefield, you must triage their ideas and offers, whilst maintaining the friendship.

Now, having said this I have been given stellar leads by some of my contacts in the past. This is because I am lucky and have made some great contacts and have some excellent business friends. But I have also had some shocking leads offered to me and had to manage them.

The best way I found to do this is to be honest with your friends. If you tell them why you don't think you will be reaching out to their potential lead, they may reveal more about it that makes you change your mind. Remember how I told you previously that the best salespeople listen more than they talk? Well, it's true in this situation too.

The fact is your business is unlikely to grow at the pace you think it will. You may have the best mousetrap, but people still don't beat a path to your door. Very quickly in your business life you run out of connections and friends to call upon and you must find leads in other ways. My rule of thumb is that if you make any sales in the first year of your business consider yourself lucky, and budget that way in your initial business plan.

Even with the most driven individuals, things take longer than you think, want, or expect them to. This is because you are selling to other people and they have different timelines, wants, needs and expectations to you. The fact is they will probably still be able to pay their mortgage and feed their families without you. They simply don't have the same urgency.

If there is, therefore, one message you should take from this text when you are starting up your business, it is plan for next to zero sales in the first year. In other words, be patient.

I get to talk to a lot of people who have started their businesses in the last ten years, almost without fail the businesses that still exist today, or have been sold to others, all saw the same thing, almost zero sales in their first year.

There are of course exceptions, we can all name them, but I think you hear about them because they are exceptions. Most businesses grind through their first year or two, simply surviving, learning, and growing, making mistakes, and correcting them or pivoting and changing their offering. If you expect that to be the case, then you will be set for success. If you can last for the first two years, the odds are you will start to grow and become a success. Not an Apple maybe, but something that in five or ten years' time will be worth several million or more and be set for its next phase of growth, or maybe disposal.

There are ways you can improve your chances of lasting through those first two years in B2B though. The first, as I have said, is demonstrate patience. Next is listen to good advice and question it. Therefore, earlier in this book I talked about taking 'smart money' from investors who really can provide help, sales connections, and sound advice. They are worth waiting for, they bring far more than money to you.

Next, use social media wisely. It isn't about scatter gunning yourself over every platform you know, you probably can't afford to do that anyway. Use social media well, provide valuable content to those people who you think will be your customers and do it regularly. Post something useful once a week on LinkedIn for example, on the same day each week. Use Twitter as a business application, in the name of your business, and share your content there, on the same day each week. Develop a pattern, be consistent, be business-like in your use of social media. You can do these things at no cost in the first instance. Openly use your connections to share and like your posts, ask them to do it. I have found that was far more valuable than the leads they 'gave' me. In this way you access their networks and the people there qualify themselves in for your goods or services. Isn't it better to have conversations with people because they reach out to you? That is where your friends and connections can truly add value to your fledgling business.

Business growth takes time, unless you have the budget of a major multi-national and can spend money on massive TV and social media campaigns. But then if you were one of those you would probably not be reading this book.

Start-ups and the 'rule of twos'

I often get the opportunity to talk to several of my peers, those people I know who were either wise enough, brave enough or stupid enough to walk away from well-paying secure jobs and throw themselves into a new venture starting their own business or being part of a start-up with others. None of them called themselves entrepreneurs, they just knew they did not want to work for somebody else and had an idea they thought would pay their mortgages and might just make them wealthy.

Many of them failed and went back to work for somebody else. Some have tried again and again, and still are. A few have been very successful and are now running healthy and profitable businesses or have sold their business and made a few lifestyle choices of their own.

Whenever I ask this last group, the successful ones, what were a few of the defining moments for them, and some of the hardest things they had to do, there was something they all had in common. They repeated the same piece of learning again and again and it's the 'rule of twos'.

I'm not going to tease you and leave you wondering until the end of this piece what this rule is, many of you may know it already, but for those of you who don't, or who are just starting out building your first business, here is what they discovered.

When, and if, your business gets to either two years old, or has annual revenues of two million dollars, pounds, or euros, it's a very good idea to seek external help at a senior level. I do not necessarily mean get additional growth funding and accept the help and advice of your funding partner, although that can be one way. I mean accept the fact that you, as the leader of your business, are probably becoming a roadblock to its continued growth and wellbeing.

Your business is probably big enough and complex enough by now to require you, as the founder and creator, to step aside and hire an experienced person and have them work as your CEO. Let them start to run your business with you. Let them help you put the strategy, organisation and processes in place that your business is already in need of in order to let it become an adult, to help it grow up and become something that is on the way to five million and above in annual revenues.

Every successful person I spoke to when I was thinking of this piece said the same thing in different ways. 'I was working twenty-hour days and still I could not answer all of the questions my people, clients, and suppliers were asking.' The more telling fact was that those people I spoke to who had failed said pretty much the same thing.

In the first year of a start-up the founder is everything, you answer the phone, make, or support, the sales calls, handle the lawyers and accountants, select and negotiate the locations, create or hire the marketing, raise and make sure the invoices are paid and a myriad of other things. Basically, you do it all and at one point it must stop, or the business will.

Most people I spoke to hired others into specific roles

such as sales and marketing, finance and many others and had them report directly to them. Those people hired in this way often found themselves waiting around to get the approval of the founder, the great 'roadblock' in the business. Many of them left the company because of that. Founders tend to be zealots, passionate control freaks, and don't believe anybody can feel about their business the way they do. The truth is they don't!

So, when you are starting up a business, and you are building your business plan make sure that as you hit that first 'two', you are allowing yourself scope to have an organisation capable of growing profitably without you filling every role in it. Remember it may be rare for people you hire to feel the same way about your business as you do, but also accept the fact that you don't know everything and let your people make decisions on behalf of the company. Step aside from the daily running of the business and trust others to help you do that. You will still work twenty-hour days, but you will be more productive and add greater value to your business. The only downside is that you will not just worry about if you can pay your mortgage, you will worry about if your staff can pay theirs... and that's the way it should be.

It can't simply be about the rule of twos, can it?
As the title of this section implies, the rule of twos is a good indicator of when to start looking and worrying about the prospects of your business, but I didn't tell you what to look out for when deciding on the exact timing of this, when to start employing professional

managers. It could be later or earlier than two years for your business.

Let me share a secret with you. I am a control freak. The day I decided to change and let the people inside the business get on and deliver the strategy was a massive eye-opener for me and the business started to grow at a much more rapid rate. But not only do you have to pick the right people, you must pick the right time.

So here are the signs to look out for in your business. If these things are happening on a regular basis, or at least too frequently to leave you with any form of comfort, then the time has come to either hire professional management or get out of the way of those you have already employed. If you don't, the best ones will leave anyway, giving you more things to worry about.

First and foremost is the situation I have already mentioned. If all decisions must come through you and things progress slowly because of it, and you spend twenty hours a day working inside your business, handling things you feel are trivial and wondering why the people you employ don't seem capable of making the simplest of decisions, well, that is the first reason to hand control over and get back to doing what you do best.

If you make decisions and nobody follows through on them with concrete actions. Well, that is sign number two. They are not following through because you have not given them the tools, information, or authority to do so normally.

If people are not growing and learning, if there is no program for helping the human resources inside your business grow and develop, well that's warning sign number three. Note, I am not saying that you must have a human resources department when you first start, but you should operate as if you do and make sure that the people you employ can see they are trusted, valued, respected and stretched. But they must have the tools, support and training to do it. So, if you operate a classic organisation with line management responsibilities, encourage, train, and allow line managers to manage and give them the resources to do so.

The previous point often leads to this next one.

If you are having trouble recruiting good people, the odds are your reputation is already 'on the street' or, at interview, your business comes across to prospective employees as dictatorial and a place where people cannot flourish. Always remember it's unlikely that people you employ will share your love and dedication to your business. They are looking for careers, they are looking at your purpose and yes, sometimes they are looking just for jobs.

If you find yourself making up policies for handling routine functions 'on the fly', and often having to revisit them or reinvent them, well the likelihood is that you have never found the time to put robust policies and practices in place, and you need to. That is one of the things professional management coming into your business will be expected to achieve early on. It's part of changing your business from a child to at least a teenager with some boundaries. It will set you on the path to make your business an adult.

The previous item, or the lack of it, generally means

that you and your people are spending a lot of your time putting out fires and never getting to the things that will help your business grow.

If you are finding yourself telling your friends what you love about your role is its variety and that every day is different and exciting, and you never get through your list of 'to-dos', well, you are probably fighting fires, and fires by their nature are destructive.

If you don't have decent accounting practices in place, and you have complaints from your bookkeeper or accountant that they can't possibly tell you what your revenues were last month, suppliers are writing to you asking for payments you thought had been made, or you are wondering why there is no cash in the company bank account even though you have produced all these goods and sold and delivered them or provided the services you promised, well, these are all signs of poor and amateur accounting practices and that is a cardinal sin in any business.

These are some of the classic signs I have seen in businesses I have been asked to help. There are others but these are the ones that are easiest to spot. By that I mean even the most egocentric entrepreneur should be able to recognise them inside their business. Look at your business and decide for yourself today, is it time I stood back a little and started to only do the things that add real value to this company?

Cash spreadsheets are king

Well, congratulations you have started your business, you have an idea, you maybe even have some product or a service you are ready to sell, you perhaps have some customers and, most importantly, you have some funding – some money either you have provided from your resources by 'bootstrapping' your business, or funding you have obtained from friends, relatives, or angel investors. You are ready to start running a real business.

First, ignore the people who tell you that you don't have a business, that you have a 'hobby'. If you have a plan, have something to sell and have formed a company, then you have a business, and it's down to you to make it work. The lifeblood of your business is cash, and people use words and phrases that are often mystical to entrepreneurs who are not financially trained. You hear words and phrases like: cash, working capital, assets, liabilities, net worth, creditors and debtors.

The fact is you will find it increasingly hard to run your business as it grows if you do not learn how a balance sheet and a profit and loss account works and, more importantly, what some of the ratios you can derive from these mean and can indicate about the health or otherwise of your business.

I know when you first have your idea and your funding you are keen to start. If you have financed your business yourself, or from friends and relatives, it could be that you have not had to think much about cash. In my experience first time entrepreneurs think more about profit. They often think of profit in rudimentary terms. They work out what their costs are and what they think they will sell, and for how much, and the difference is profit. They are part of the way to buying their superyacht as the profits from their business come rolling in, at least in their heads they are.

If you don't know already, although profit is very important it is far from the most important thing about the finances of your business. That award, the 'Oscar' of business, in my opinion, goes to cash. I truly believe that cash is king and if you run out of cash you can have a very 'profitable' business that is forced into a sale, or another round of fund raising at a much lower share price, or into bankruptcy, simply because you forgot the one fundamental about your business. That cash is what makes it exist. Now, I know you will all be saying 'No, the customer is king', and they are, but this is about financing and running your business. I'm assuming for the sake of this that you have happy customers who want to buy more of what you are offering.

My strong advice, therefore, is, before you do anything, when you are first starting, build a spreadsheet or use those provided as part of your online business banking app that details your cash flow. A pretty good and useful one is provided for free by Microsoft for you to use in Excel. Use this to build a cash flow forecast. We all know it's your best guess at this stage, but go twelve months forward in your business and put in those 'best guesses'. What this exercise will do is show you how much cash you should have in hand in your bank account at the end of each month of trading. This is your plan, and don't do it and then put it away in a folder on your laptop called 'plans'. This spreadsheet is going to be one of the most valuable tools you will use to run your business in your first year, and every year it exists until you exit and buy that yacht.

Every single month, as a bare minimum, replace the plan numbers in that spreadsheet with your actual results and add another month of forecast numbers to it as well. See what it does to your future bank balance for each month.

Some businesses I know do this on a weekly basis, but I would advise you to spend the right amount of time on this exercise, and you will know what is right from experience as you progress. If there are other people in your business then share that cash flow spreadsheet with them too, let them see what impact their efforts are having on the business. I'm not a fan of secrecy and 'need to know'. I believe people work best when they are trusted, respected and informed.

One of the simple measures I used to use in the businesses I jointly owned or led was simply to look at my cash position for this year compared to the same point last year. For me that was a very good measure of growth and health in the business. If there are differences either up or down, you should be able to rationalise or explain them. While we are on that subject, if you are doing that, don't lie to yourself, don't make excuses, it's a dumb person who believes their own lies after all.

Anyway, back to running your business and your cash flow spreadsheet. I used to use mine to help me set a few rules in my business, such as how much cash I always wanted to keep easily available to the business. In my case it was often three months of operating expenditure. I reasoned this because if I saw problems developing that I had to act upon it would often take three months to see the effects of those actions ripple through my business. Typically, if we had orders for the future, those orders that were going to provide cash to the bank account were certain three months into the future, so I had a very good idea of how much cash was coming into my business over the coming three months.

The cash flow spreadsheet has many ways it can help you run your business, but most of all it is an operational tool. It does have some hidden gems in it though, and, because it's a spreadsheet, it enables you to play with various ideas. It enables you to model your business and even look at sensitivities inside your business. If, for example, you are running short of cash in four months' time, can you bring some orders forward? Can you negotiate extended payment terms with your suppliers? Can you promote certain items of your stock to your clients swapping a discounted price for faster payment? Are your clients taking too long to pay you, what would be the effect on your business of offering prompt payment discounts? You can model all these scenarios and a host more using a good cash flow spreadsheet.

Focus for now on cash and treasure it. It is there to be used, to help you grow your business, to buy stock, to market your business, to pay your staff and suppliers, to keep you growing. It is an asset, learn to know what you have, learn to know what you will have and, with that knowledge, make informed business decisions.

A wise management accountant who worked with me in several companies said to me once, 'I can make profit in this business be almost anything that suits what we are doing, but cash, I can't hide what cash shows us and I would never want to.' It's good advice.

Experimenting in your business

I was brought up on a diet of experimentation and investigation. Research scientists postulate theories and then design experiments to try and prove them. When they find their idea is incorrect, they log the data and keep it. It helps them eliminate other theories as well and thus speeds the research process. It's the same things doctors do when they are trying to diagnose your illness. They order a battery of tests on your body aimed at eliminating the possible illnesses you may have. The best diagnosticians do this from a mix of experience, probability and learning. They get to the problem quickly and at lowest cost.

Now, as a founder in your business, do you do that?

When you have a great idea for a new product or a new service in your growing business and it doesn't work, what do you do? Do you say, 'I will learn from that and not make the same mistake' then you go and do something similar that fails a few months later? Don't feel bad, many people do and it's for a very simple reason. It's because of what you focus on when you have a new idea.

Most people when they are growing their business and they are either trying something new or making a slight pivot into a new or related area, focus on what the outcome will be. They have in their minds what success will look like and get very excited about how they will invest or spend the money the new idea will realise for them. I think this is wrong.

When you have a new idea for a product or service, and you are looking at how to launch it, I would suggest only launching it in a way that if it succeeds or fails you will truly learn from the experience. If you are making an investment, pick only those that will generate value for your business, irrespective if it is a success or failure. Most business owners only think of the hoped for outcome, the success. I would suggest that the best business owners look for the opportunity to learn on the journey to success or failure and they design their investments to do just this.

To do this, you must spend the time to think about all the potential outcomes of the initiative, not just the big prize or the worst failure. There will be many outcomes that fall between these two extremes. You need to design your work program to allow you to capture the most value from the investment you are making.

A simple example of this comes in digital marketing. Yes, all those Google ads, LinkedIn feeds and posts, Twitter promotions, Facebook ads and all the other things that pop up all over our journey through the internet.

Many times, I have seen businesses waste huge sums on digital advertising simply through lack of planning. They often don't even work out how much each lead they obtain using digital marketing is worth in terms of its lifetime value and then don't spend appropriately to give themselves the best chance of securing those top leads. Or worse, they spend to their budget and, because the budget is insufficient, they get poor leads or very few leads to work on and convert into clients and declare 'digital marketing doesn't work'.

I see businesses pay scant attention to things like their website visitors and the conversion rates of these visits into desirable outcomes. Ask your marketing teams what the aim of each page of their website is and what are they doing in terms of an integrated approach to social media to drive conversions from that web page. The answer may surprise you.

I used to believe in the old phrase 'I know I am wasting half of my marketing budget, but I don't know which half'. I don't think that is true anymore. Or if it is then you are doing your marketing, and especially your digital marketing, badly.

Let me share some of the things I discovered when I first started using digital marketing because I was working with a group of people who helped me design the experiment I was running.

I learnt that.

- Human beings speaking draw attention to your communication, video sells.
- Consumers are far more sophisticated than I had ever believed.
- It doesn't matter what the picture is in an advert (if it is not tasteless or illegal), it just must be bright and have lots of colour.
- The day you post your advertisement really does matter, as does the time when it is seen.
- I did not have an idea that made people excited.
- My offering was not understood the way I was explaining it.
- My first offering was not the one that most people

wanted, and I wasn't charging for the things people valued most.

Value was even more important than clever content.
All these learnings came from one or two business initiatives that we recognised were failures, but the learning experiences they gave us made our next initiatives very successful. So much so we started to grow the business at double the rate we had previously been doing.

Good design of new initiatives and taking the time to ensure you collect valuable and relevant data along the journey is crucial to the success of your business, and this is the mind set you need to instil in everything you do. If you do this even your 'failures' are successes.

Scaling a business is a skill not an accident

I am a self-confessed zealot when it comes to customer service. I like to think that the clients of the companies I ran saw that and enjoyed what it brought them.

Being such a zealot is difficult though, it brings you angst, and when you see examples of other organisations failing to deliver it hurts, especially when you are the recipient of poor service.

In the last few years, myself and my wife have often been the victim of poor service, and in examining the worst offenders they seem to be those companies that are either in monopolistic positions or struggling to scale. And scaling successfully is a skill that businesses need to acquire.

Today gave me another example of some awful

service I received from one such company. What was amazing is that they failed me when I was spending more money with them!

Anyway, the marketing hype had got to me, and I decided to replace my existing quite large subscription set up with a bigger offering using their latest technology. Online ordering was easy and the promise of the engineer who would be doing the installation staying to show us how to use it and get the best from it sounded like a company who cared and wanted to add value. I should have known things were not all they seemed when I tried to book the appointment at the time of ordering and discovered I would have to wait for four weeks for the installation, but at least I was given an 8 am to 1 pm time slot. At 12.37 pm on the day, I received a text saying that due to circumstances beyond their control they would not be turning up today and they had rebooked my appointment for 30th October, eight days away! They did give me a number to call if I needed to speak to them and said that, as recompense, they had added a 25 GBP credit to my account.

Well, I did need to speak to them, because the 30th October was not convenient. After negotiating a terrible voice driven call guardian, talking to somebody who could not help me, who redirected my call but failed to tell the next person in line who I was, that I had been through the security questions once already, and what my issue was, I worked my way through to a second human. Now that human was very pleasant and apologetic but didn't know why an engineer had failed to turn up. He told me that if the 30th October was not convenient then the next available appointment was on 17th November, fifty-five days after I placed the order. I was stunned. In the end I agreed to change my diary and my life and now the engineer was meant to be coming to me on the 30th October.

AND then it got very silly. Two hours later I received an email from the company, confirming my new appointment, and apart from mentioning that I was going to get what I ordered, I would also be getting their broadband and voice telephony service, two things I had not even ordered, and I certainly didn't want!

So, it was time to get back onto the phone, again the call guardian, the poor routing and telling the whole sorry tale to somebody else, who had to go away and talk to someone else and left me hanging on the phone for another couple of minutes, without even a version of 'Greensleeves' to listen to. Eventually they explained that the email was a standard document (it implied that the recipient had also ordered broadband and voice telephony) and everybody gets it who ordered what I had, but could I make sure that my own broadband service was working when the engineer arrived, oh, and by the way, 'your order does not include broadband and voice telephony, you can ignore that'.

It's simply a rubbish way to deal with clients, and it's becoming all too common as companies think they can automate, outsource, systematise and generally short cut the process of scaling their business.

Scaling a business is a skill, and few people do it well, but applying some thought to it and learning from your mistakes, truly empowering staff and not 'compartmentalising' decision making or customer care are some of the fundamentals that must be got right.

To scale well you do need great processes and excellent systems, but most of all you need highly motivated, well-rewarded and well-trained staff who are encouraged and allowed to put the customer first and make decisions.

If I was running the company in question, and I was letting clients down, I would not rely upon text messages, systems and call centres. I would make sure a human rang the client as soon as possible, told them the reason for letting them down, offered them a choice of new appointments and finally closed with the fact that, by way of compensation, they would like to offer the client something that was of value to them.

That would take one person in the organisation five or maybe ten minutes. The client would feel valued and, in my experience, even the most upset individual would find it hard to scream and yell for more than the first minute of the call.

I spoke to three different people for at least ten to fifteen minutes each that day. The current approach must cost the company more in time, money and goodwill than my suggested approach. It certainly cost me more time than five minutes... and now I am sharing with you just how bad my experience of them was. It is true, a happy customer tells at least five people, and an unhappy one tells twenty, or in my case just over one thousand, or more!

Too many businesses play at customer service and look to maximise profits and scale at any speed or, seemingly, cost, and that is a serious mistake.

A key measure when you are scaling your business is customer churn, I wonder what this company's would be if they had some serious competition, especially in the more rural areas of the world.

When you need more cash

I'm starting to see the fallout of the COVID-19 pandemic with several early-stage growth companies and some SMEs contacting me for the first time asking for help. Largely their immediate problem is cash. Basically, it is time for them to raise some cash, assuming the business is viable. What follows are some ideas and advice about how to go about doing this, and a warning.

First, I encourage them to look at their cash flow statements thoroughly; this will help them decide if the situation is likely to be temporary or more permanent and direct them in the actions to be taken.

If the problem is temporary, it may well be that it can be resolved with a short-term loan. Right now, through most of the world, money is relatively cheap, and in some cases it is close to free as Governments continue to support industry with very favourable loans. But if this is not an option then you need to secure short-term cash in other ways. If you are a small business, just starting, you may find your initial investors are willing to lend you money, for a minimal rate of return. I would advise against issuing more shares if you can avoid it. Not only does this take time and cost you more money, but you could also find some of your early-stage investors becoming disheartened with an early dilution of their investment, especially if they are not able to subscribe to another share issue earlier than they expected to.

Assuming you are not so small that you are tempted to fund your cash flow crisis using your credit cards (I always wince when I hear people doing this), then you are probably going to have to go to your bank. Here there will likely be two options. An overdraft facility, or a longer-term loan, for which the bank will look to secure their investment against some form of asset, such as your own property, or with guarantees of some type from yourself, fellow directors, or shareholders. At this stage things are serious, and I am so often amazed by the cases for the loan that business owners put forward. So many simply don't do the work that is needed and the meeting with their bank results in a refusal and frustration.

So here comes the warning I mentioned earlier. Take the application for the loan very seriously or it will fail. I have seen the fallout of the 'easy money' that some companies have been able to secure from banks that are backed by government schemes. Many company owners seem to think that the way the banks operated at that part of the pandemic is the way they always will. They forget that the loans the banks were offering then were secured by the government. Loans they are issuing now must be managed in the old way, as a risk they are looking for a reward from. Remember, issuing loans and gaining from them is what banks are in business for. That is their business model, and most have proven to be very good at it. Assuming you put aside the financial crisis of the mid-2000s.

So, prepare well for the application, and what I mean

by this is make sure you back your application by several things.

- A history of the company, including an outline of the business operations.
- A statement of today's market conditions for your sector and its prospects for the future. Be conservative because you are likely to be challenged.
- A robust and accurate cash flow forecast for your business, including any expansion plans you have and including the way that you will be able to service the debt that will result from a successful loan application. Again, be conservative. If you are perceived as being unrealistic or over-optimistic it will harm your case.
- Present copies of your previous accounts ready for the bank to consider.
- Include details of your company's key personnel and I would suggest also providing a cap table to show who owns shares in your company.

In doing this you will be rehearsing your own case. It will help you recognise the strengths and weaknesses in your arguments. Remember that if one bank refuses you there are others, but I would suggest that you approach them in a serial manner, not asking several for the same loan. All will do credit checks on your business and multiple credit checks taking place on your business can be harmful. Patience and preparation are the key and if you receive a refusal find out why and try and correct that aspect of your business or presentation before your next application.

If you are looking for a more permanent solution to your cash flow issues and need an injection of working capital to either stay alive or expand, there are many other ways to do this. Some of those I have seen and been part of include:

- If you own your business premises, you may consider a sale and lease back arrangement. This means selling your building to a pension fund or insurance company who are seeking assets such as that. The company then leases the property back to you for an agreed term and rent. They gain the capital value of the asset and a steady income whilst you continue to use it and create working capital for your business.

- Sometimes it can be wise at these times to evaluate your business and look to dispose part of it to another company. Common ways to identify parts of your business to do this to are those that no longer fit your product line or marketing strategy. But if you are doing this it is critical to ensure that it can clearly be defined as an autonomous part of your business and that its divestment will not result in the demise of your whole business. It is often the case that a business that no longer suits you will be a real asset to another company who may be looking for revenue expansion, new markets to enter or cross-selling opportunities.

- You may have an asset in your business which is no longer making a reasonable percentage return for the capital you have invested in it and the future costs to maintain it. This should be considered for disposal and may result in more effective business practices and processes. I always advise owners to be both ruthless and realistic when considering this option and consider the consequences of being without this asset, or the cost of replacing it. Just because something is not making money for you does not mean that others cannot use it effectively. Often pieces of manufacturing equipment or storage facilities can fall into this category.

- You may decide to raise capital from both existing and new shareholders. I mentioned this earlier as something to avoid when looking for a temporary cash injection. Share issues are not to be taken lightly. They do mean, of course, that you gain cash for simply the cost of administering the share issue itself, but it means you are diluting existing shareholders when they cannot or do not wish to maintain their percentage holding in the company. This is likely to include yourself. In my opinion share issues are best done when they are being done for a positive reason, usually company expansion. When they are done to provide cash to keep a business running not only are they harder to complete, you are likely to come under pressure for the share price investors paid last to be higher than the share price you will achieve now, creating a 'down round' which will stay with your business. If you decide to take this approach you once again must prepare well, just as you did for the application for a bank loan.

In summary, rarely does any business go through its life without at some time feeling cash pressures. You can be very profitable but still be forced into closure or bankruptcy due to a lack of cash in your accounts, unable to pay your staff costs and suppliers. It is for this reason that cash inside your business has to be managed. But it is just that, an asset to be managed. There are many other ways than those I have described above to provide a cash injection into your business. The ones I have mentioned are those I have seen in operation or been part of. Your circumstances will be unique and you and your fellow directors and shareholders, along with your bankers, must make the right decisions for your business. I don't advocate any approach listed here above the others, but all are worth considering. If you are struggling to decide, always take expert advice and be prepared for some unpalatable truths to surface, it's one of the pleasures and strains of running a business.

When you need to, but you can't cut costs

I often find myself called in to help companies reduce their costs in the early stages of their existence, when cash is dwindling away and they don't want to dilute shareholder value with another raise, at possibly a lower price, or they don't want, or cannot obtain, loans.

Very often the founders tell me that they have done all the cost-cutting they can, that they have looked at price rises, or volume increases, and they have carried out a thorough expense analysis of their business.

At these times I tend to go back to what is simply good practice. These things apply to all businesses, not just start-ups. I do find start-ups are often the worst offenders in some of these areas though, and by paying attention they can manage their cash flow through the leaner times before their growth really kicks in.

I concentrate on a few areas, and I question people hard to make sure they both understand the implications of these areas and have done everything they can to get as efficient with their cash as possible.

I start in two areas, their cash collection and their payments to suppliers. I check the following:

- Do they have written agreements with clients in place that are clear and unambiguous?
- Do they carry out credit checks and references on new clients?
- Do they invoice promptly and accurately?
- Do they provide, and get agreement about, their terms and their collection policies and stick to them?
- Do they keep an aged debtors list and follow up promptly when payments have been missed or are late?
- Are they taking advantage of all trade discounts offered to them, for instance those involving payment schedules?
- Do they pay their bills strictly 'to terms'? In other words, do they pay bills only when they are due?
- Are they simply keeping accurate and timely records in their business and identifying easy to understand and effective key performance indicators (KPIs) for their business?
- Do they have robust purchasing processes that are fast and easy to use whilst still ensuring that purchasing practices adhere to policy and established contracts?
- Do they regularly seek to gain extended credit terms

with their suppliers and other creditors? As they get more established these will improve and they should take advantage of their good payment history or increased volumes.

- Do they buy inventory only when they need it?
- Do they question the logic of 'bulk purchasing' deals they are committed to?
- Have they investigated the option of 'bartering' with other trade partners to reduce levels of older stock, or indeed seek new markets?

Another common area where slippage can occur that will cost them money is around inventory:

- Do they regularly review their inventory holding policies? Do they look at their stock turnover rate to see if they can reduce stocks whilst maintaining customer service levels?
- Are their security policies and activities sound, are they preventing theft by their own staff?
- Are their employees trained in the handling of the product? Are damages and losses too high or worse, increasing?
- How are they handling and accounting for goods that are returned to them? Are these being processed efficiently and returned to good stock that can be resold?

In the area of production:

- Can they reduce changeover times between stock items, or can they schedule production better to manage the levels of inventory they hold?

- Have they effectively tendered for the goods and services they buy from suppliers to ensure they are getting the best prices from them whilst maintaining or improving quality?
- Have they worked with their suppliers to obtain products in a format that will reduce the time it takes in preparing for their use in their production facilities? Are the unit/pack sizes right for them so that they can both handle these and they are not compelled to buy more than they need?
- Are they maintaining their quality and making product or services that are 'right first time' to reduce rehandling?
- Are they eliminating unprofitable products or services from their offering?
- Are they committed to maintaining good relationships with their suppliers whilst challenging the logic of their pricing?
- Are they looking at the design of their products to reduce costs whilst maintaining or improving quality?
- Are they looking at the option of outsourcing all or some of their manufacturing process regularly?
- Are they investigating the option of suppliers holding stocks at no cost to them and only assuming title to the goods when they enter their factory gate?

In the area of marketing and sales:
- Is their marketing laser focussed rather than scatter gun? Do they know how to target their most profitable clients and use a marketing approach which is targeted to them alone?

- Do they police and ensure that any discounting they agree to works and achieves the results it is intended to deliver?
- Do they train all customer-facing staff in the skill of 'upselling' where they can offer extended goods or services to clients based upon what they have already purchased? Are their staff trained and empowered to do this?
- Do they train their staff in customer contact and record and document clearly all customer interactions? Do they have and police a high standard of quality and satisfaction as a cultural norm in their company when dealing with clients?
- Do they ensure that every staff member recognises that they have clients that are both external and internal?

In hiring and personnel:
- What are their recruitment plans? Do they have to hire, or can they cover the need in the short-term by overtime working? Can they in fact use subcontractors or freelance staff, or maybe even part-time workers?
- How frequently do they pay their staff? Do all staff have to be paid on the same day?
- How effectively is their factory or process running? Is downtime causing staffing levels to be higher than the optimum?
- Are starting and finishing times being adhered to, the same question should be asked of break times for meals and rest?

- Is 'petty cash' usage increasing with no apparent reason? This can often indicate either theft or, more likely, the purchasing of items out of policy, or outside of negotiated agreements.

I have never found a company that is excellent in all these areas.

Each one of these areas has a direct impact on a company's cash position and its future wellbeing. Use this section of the book as a checklist when times are tough to help you through the stickiest of patches. It really does work.

Growth at all costs

So, is it better to go all out for growth, or better to get established and then grow?

I know that, when I'm asked that by people, the answer I give will be wrong. All I tell them is the way I like to grow businesses is to get established, and then go for rapid growth. I like to be sure that the product or service the business is offering is a good fit to the market it is trying to address. Going all out for rapid growth straight away, in my opinion, deflects from that.

I have seen a few examples of businesses that have really gone for growth early in their lives and have failed. One was a food business, aimed at the UK consumer. They were fortunate and were able to introduce a new product to a single major UK retailer. The product was novel and the consumer appeared to love it. The retailer in question saw its potential, saw the product flying from the shelves and, within weeks, was doubling and trebling orders to the manufacturer. They were not ready to meet the demand being created, they did not have funding in place to scale, and in fact had no real plan to be able to produce the product in the large quantities that was now being required of them. Their company failed because they tried to scale too fast. A major food manufacturer entered the market twelve months later with a competitive offering and the capability to produce their product at the scale demanded by the UK food retailers.

This is an example of the way some businesses choose their market. They choose to try and sell to companies that are too big for their capabilities. Going all out for rapid growth, without considering the issues that come from scaling. Had they started, perhaps, by selling their product online, or in smaller independent stores, they could have learnt more about their product, their business, their market and how to scale production before approaching the UK retailers with a product that was clearly a winning proposition. When the large orders came flooding in, they would have been set with the funding required and the knowledge of how to produce their product at the scale the market demanded.

Another example I know of, where the owners of the business are providing in store services to the clients of a UK retailer, had opted for a different approach. They are now growing rapidly, but in a controlled manner hand in hand with the retailer in question. They are working in partnership with the retailer. They developed a formula with them that they were able to test in one of two of the retailer's stores. They refined their business model and their delivery, taking the time to match their service to the market before starting to scale. Now they can deliver success after success in every one of the retailer's stores they enter with this service. They have a proven well-tried model that works. They know their costs and they know the formula to follow. Every in-store unit they place goes into profit within a year of its establishment. They took their time, they matched their offering to the market, refining it from the experience they gained until they had a formula that was a guaranteed success. They continue to refine it still and they ensure that lessons learnt are transferred across their business. They had a plan and had discussed it with their major client before promising to deliver things they simply could not, as the food manufacturer I talked about did.

Very often founders seem to take every sale that is at available to them, finding themselves being taken into blind alleys with little long-term growth prospects simply because they believe that there is no such thing as a 'bad sale' when you are starting up. I would always advise testing each opportunity against the strategy you should have built, and preferably a set of milestones you had set yourself as well. I am not, by this statement, saying that you should not 'pivot' your business, or not follow opportunities, that is part of finding your market. But you should follow these sales with your eyes open and, if you feel you are deviating from your strategic direction, you should question it and be very sure that it is a good move for the business and take steps to give your business the best chance of success, even if this means negotiating a phased approach with your clients.

When I led a business called Freight Traders, one of the first online logistics platforms back in 1999, our first model was to run online freight auctions for single loads of freight. It used the power of the internet and the free market to match freight owners with the carriers who owned the trucks capable of moving their loads. We targeted the biggest freight owners and the biggest truck operators in the UK at first with a view that we would massively improve an inefficient market. (About 27 per cent of load capacity in the UK was empty at any one time back in 1999.) It worked well for small cargo owners and small trucking companies, but it was not the way that major manufacturers purchased the movement of their goods. They wanted to have longer-term contracts, for moving multiple loads over different geographies. Had we tried to scale using our initial business model and market fit, we would have failed. We changed the software to match our desired market, running a series of massive freight tenders for Europe's largest manufacturers, no longer looking to run a high volume of single load freight auctions, but using the software to facilitate strategic buying by Europe's largest manufacturers. When we made this change the business started to grow at a much faster rate, but it took us 15 months to truly find this out.

In talking to a few fellow investors and some of the venture capitalists I know, they seem to agree with me. They like to see a coherent idea from founders that is refined to match a real market before they see their money spent on expensive advertising to a market that doesn't exist. Or worse, the examples I saw in the dot-com boom where vast sums of money were burnt by founders, especially in the software industry, on advertising and promoting 'vapour ware', software that was conceptual rather than real, and rarely delivered against its promise.

If you follow this advice, it's true you may end up losing first mover advantage, you may become a 'me too' type product or offering, but if the market is real and either is, or can be made, big enough, there will be enough revenue for you and many competitors. You will benefit from them helping you grow the market by spending their advertising dollars as well. A steady, and perhaps conservative, approach helps you minimise risk to yourself and your investors. It helps you sell your vision to your next round of investors or reinforces your plan to your original angel investors and thus should help you raise additional funds more easily. Finally, it helps your product or service gain traction in the market the best way it possibly can, by being talked about by happy clients. In my view, word of mouth and social media 'buzz' is still the best and lowest cost way I know of creating a successful business.

I like to quote Amazon to people. They didn't rush. They started in July 1994 as an online bookseller, they became one of the largest online retailers in the world and developed a very large and lucrative business as part of these activities, providing web services through AWS to the world's businesses. Steady, measured progress seemed to work for them.

Some truths and tips about scaling your business

A good question, that was asked by many of the people I work with, and mentor is how do I handle scaling the business from a handful of enthusiastic entrepreneurs to a business with twenty, thirty or fifty people?

My personal view is that the two most important components to making a success of this phase in your business growth are people and processes. These are closely followed by communication.

First, let's talk about one of the hardest parts of running a business when you are scaling. That is the fact that some of your fellow entrepreneurs might simply be incapable of achieving this.

Some of your fellow founders may be great as entrepreneurs and founders but frankly a disaster when a business starts to grow. It is not uncommon for some individuals to be magical generalists who can get things done and think on their feet.

These people thrive in the early days of a business, when nobody has job titles or defined responsibilities, but they stop performing when the business grows and their jobs become narrower. It could also be that they simply were fortunate to be along for the ride when the business started and provided great value to it then, but their value has diminished. As a founder and leader, you need to be strong enough, and open enough, to recognise this, and be capable of having the hard conversation with them that terminates their employment with the company.

They will probably retain their shares of course, and they will have had a great experience, but their capabilities simply don't match what the business needs as it grows and they would stifle its growth. Keeping them as employees is a mistake for the business, for you and for the other founders. It can be messy and emotional but partings do have to take place in most businesses that are scaling in my experience. As a friend of mine said so well to me one day, 'It is important to close the door on these people quietly.' Part as friends and colleagues with a clear understanding of why this has had to happen, and leaving the door ajar for them to come back in perhaps a new role, being part of a new division or a new initiative in a few years' time. If you are scaling well and they retain their shares in the original business, you will be making them wealthy anyway.

The next thing that I tell people is that, at this stage in the business's life, it is moving from childhood, through adolescence, into becoming an adult. The analogy I always use is to think of children playing football. When they are between three and six years old, typically every person on the team races towards the ball determined to get a kick and move it towards the opponent's goal. It is chaos, but it is fun, and the stronger team usually is the one that wins, often they simply last longer.

As the children age, between the ages of 6 and 14 they start to realise that better opportunities arise to score when they are spaced out, when they start to occupy different areas of the pitch and they are able to pass the ball to each other and that sometimes it's perfectly acceptable for you to spend time without the ball, but be available and in the right position to get it passed to you.

When the team gets to 15 and into adulthood, they start to occupy specialist roles, they understand how their role fits into the team, and they do everything they can to do their role in the best possible way. They hold their fellow team mates to account and support them when they are having a bad game or are injured. They recognise for the first time that their opponents are trying to do the same to them, in the same way, to beat them and to dominate them. Your team needs to win and to do this, for the first time, you employ strategy, tactics and processes.

So how do you turn your business into an adult?

My view is that you use processes to do that. Much as entrepreneurs often hate processes they need to begin, they need to be documented and they need to be in place. But I can hear you groaning, 'This is bureaucracy, and it is feeling like the business I left because you could get nothing done, I don't want to recreate that.' My answer to that is simple. This is YOUR business, think about what you are doing and build processes for the things that are essential to your customers' wellbeing. Have good ways to take orders, have good ways to deliver to and support the customer, have good ways to collect your cash and have good ways to measure the financial progress your business is making. Focus on those external areas and, as you manage this external interface, make sure you have processes to look after the growing number of people you are introducing to your business. Develop good processes to protect the health, safety, and wellbeing of your people. Develop good processes to onboard them into your business and introduce them to the culture of the business. You want to create new employees that think and feel the way that your best founders do, but bring their own skill set and experience to the business too. If your new processes don't work, be agile enough to change them, involve your small workforce in designing the processes and only ever blame yourself if your business processes don't do what they are meant to, or introduce too much bureaucracy into your business. After all you don't need to bring 'corporate thinking' into your small business, and if you do who can you blame for that? Processes are what make businesses grow into adulthood.

Now I want to talk about a third topic, the importance of communication inside your business. It's a massive topic but I will highlight two areas. Helping people become engaged with the business and behaviour inside your organisation.

One way I found that people became very engaged with the businesses I led was by sharing key company data with them. I always insisted that everybody inside the business would get a monthly report that showed how the business was performing financially. I am amazed still by the number of growing businesses that don't do this. Some founders appear to feel that this is sharing with strangers how wealthy, or perhaps poor, they are getting. I have heard statements like 'If they see we are doing so well they will all be asking for pay rises', or 'If they see we are struggling I will lose all the best people I have', even better 'If they see how much money we are taking in dividends they will all want to get increased bonuses'. When I hear those kinds of statements I truly worry. They show me that the owners of the business seem to think that information is power or have something to hide. They seem to forget that if they become a public business their accounts would be public information anyway, and often in much more detail than a simple monthly 'how we are doing' report sent to all staff would show.

For me this is a matter of trust. Showing how the business is doing to everybody in it shows that the founders and owners trust their people to use the information they are given in the right way. If your business is doing well, then reward your staff well. In these reports show them how they are making progress towards the company-wide bonuses you should pay for exceptional results. If the business is struggling, don't you trust your people to help you change that situation? In my experience, when people see and understand a problem they try and do something to resolve it. If you lose a few people because of doing this, well to be honest they were probably the people you wanted to lose anyway.

The type of financial report I am suggesting is not huge, and the information needs to be easily digestible. I have told you before, I was very fortunate in having the best management accountant I have ever known work with me in two of the businesses I ran. He produced monthly financial reports that enabled even the most financially illiterate person inside the business to understand its health. He did this using a mixture of trend graphs that included plan and reforecast lines as well as actuals. In some areas he compared this year's numbers with those of last year and he also used a moving annual average approach to financial numbers which he explained simply to people as, 'If the business stopped today this would be the result of our last twelve months of trading.'

These reports included sales revenues and costs, and our current and predicted cash positions. They did not talk about profits, they can be manipulated. The reports showed the key parameters that people could act on without recourse to anybody else. The report was always accompanied by a short number of notes to highlight areas that were things to celebrate and those things that were warning signals. The last business I ran was an international one and we divided the world into three regions, this report helped to 'gamify' the business performance and it was always a subject of amusement and challenges between the respective geographic teams. The business also had two types of revenue, subscription licences and the provision of services. We had a strategy to make this an 80/20 split and the report also showed how we were performing against this. If we borrowed money, and sometimes we did, we showed this money on our cash statements, people knew exactly how much the company had in the bank at the end of each month and could see the forecast for the future. Our sales team was incredibly realistic about the deals they thought would close in the future and we only included those deals we had signatures for in our forward cash estimates.

In this way we made sure everybody in the business

'bought into' the financial performance of the business they were driving, and they owned it. When we paid them bonuses, they saw the dip in cash it caused, and they knew that cash was the lifeblood of the business.

The second thing I want to talk about in terms of communication is the things most people think of most of all. The communications of the leaders to everybody inside the business. I am a great advocate of having a monthly 'town hall' meeting, as the unicorns of Silicon Valley like to call it. For me it should consist of the founder talking through the highlights of the financial report the employees have in their hands and it should be a meeting to which everybody is invited. It should talk about how the business is performing against its strategic plan and it should talk about the things the founders or leadership team are thinking about and working on. It doesn't need showcase presentations from different parts of the business as the norm, but it should allow initiatives of high relevance to be shown. Such as how great a major new release is within a software business. Sometimes it's also good to invite a marquee client along to talk about what you are doing for their business. The key is to inform employees and let them ask questions of you, and with Zoom and other technologies it is easy to do now.

The other part of communication I want to highlight is a much darker side. It is the simple fact that in your business, if you are a founder and a leader, you set the tone of what is acceptable behaviour. If you are a bully, treat people badly and steamroller your way through each day because you see that as acceptable behaviour and it is your way of showing you are 'driven', then remember that you are demonstrating to all the people inside your business that this is the acceptable way. People working directly for you will start to treat their staff the same way, your behaviour is quickly reflected throughout the organisation. This is an important point and poor leaders often pay the least attention to it. So, think hard about your own style and what you are conveying and illustrating as the way to behave, because what you do other people will try to mimic, often with people who are far less resilient to aggressive behaviour than they themselves are. You will soon lose your best people and create a toxic atmosphere.

CHAPTER 7 – ON EXITS, VALUATIONS AND INVESTORS

The journey is nearly complete, until the next business you start after your first successful exit.

To make it through to this point you will have been involved in many of the things that I have spoken about earlier in the book. You will have survived your first two years, grown, marketed, sold things and bought things. You will have scaled and survived the cash crises that often hit new or growing businesses.

This chapter is mainly about how you prepare your business for sale and what you are likely to go through when managing a due diligence process. But it also contains some advice about how to manage your investors and a basic introduction to how company valuations are communicated and the dilutive effect they have on you and other shareholders. You may be surprised how quickly the value of the shares you have in a healthy business grow, and how dilution with a new valuation can appear to be a magic means by which your personal wealth grows if you handle it correctly.

When it's time to leave or cash out

I have said earlier that, when I am asked to invest in a start-up or early-stage business, one of the things I want to see is a clear plan for an exit. After all, if I am going to put my money in your business, I want to be assured that you and I are both aligned in terms of how I will get my money back out of your business. I'm not investing for fun, I'm investing to help both of us increase our wealth.

One of the most common exits for business owners is of course a sale of some sort, either to a competitor or to a third party who sees the opportunities in your business that they can exploit, and thus increase their investment. Some of you will go on to take your company public and sell shares to the masses.

In either of these cases people tend to look for the same things from your business, and although when you are first starting up some of these seem a 'pipe dream', your strategic plan should be looking to deliver a business with a unique set of attributes that make it investible.

I have seen these best expressed in a recent book by Peter Seilern, a fund manager with over fifty years' experience. The book is called *Only the Best Will Do* and in it Peter lays out his rules that have to be passed in order for him to invest.

My feeling is few businesses truly have all of these, but when you are building your business and growing, you should have one eye towards achieving all of these if you can.

Firstly, he talks about having a scalable business model. You must be able to take your early-stage business, where you treat each customer like royalty, and be able to do that with a much larger number. I talked about how to help this happen in the previous section. If you can't scale, I would suggest that you don't have something you can call a business... after all even football agents generally have more than one client!

Something that will attract investors, or buyers, is if

you show superior growth to other businesses in your sector. You often see this with software businesses. There are lots of very good ideas, but often only one or two in a sector that grow faster than others. Try to be one of those, and this doesn't mean that you have to be first.

Industry leadership is important. To be seen as the business in your industry who is truly the knowledge leader, who innovates and delivers a superior customer experience is worth money. It helps you become the growth leader and maybe your name will one day become synonymous with the task you deliver. After all, in the UK very few people vacuum their houses, they still 'hoover' them, and I have heard nobody say they 'Dyson' their homes. Having said that Hoover still exists but it is no longer the first name people in the UK talk about when buying a vacuum cleaner. They lost the innovation race.

Another big plus is if you can demonstrate a sustainable competitive advantage. To be the business who is the leader, to be the business who others aspire to be. But most of all to be the business that it would take large investment and many years to topple from your position of superiority. This is the 'moat' that Warren Buffett is famed for referring to.

Something else investors like is that you can demonstrate strong organic growth. That you market, sell and scale your offering. That you develop new markets, services or products from your own resources and make them successful. This is not to say that acquisitions are not a good way to grow, but very many acquisitions fail to deliver their promised benefits. So they should be very well considered and researched. After all, investors or potential buyers will look to see how easy you have found it to acquire and integrate other businesses.

If your business can demonstrate a wide geographic coverage, or a wide customer diversification, this is also a plus point. What this simply means is that you have a large addressable market and are not a niche business. Now, having said this, many niche businesses are very successful, but often because they have many of the other attributes I have already discussed. Put simply, you want to be able to sell to as many buyers as possible, but without overstretching your resources by needless unprofitable expansion.

If you are looking at building a business, capital, the amount of money it takes you to develop and run your business, is of course important. In the book, Peter favours businesses with low capital intensity. In other words, businesses that invest low amounts of money for every dollar they generate in revenues. So that means if you are thinking of making the next best automobile, well, you had better be very sure you are going to sell a lot of them. Whilst on the subject of capital, you would be wise to keep a very good eye on the return you get for the capital you employ in your business. The Return on Capital Employed (ROCE). A high value indicates that you can eventually return larger amounts of money to the shareholders of the company. If your ROCE is consistently high, then it is likely the profits you reinvest in your business rather than pay as dividends to shareholders lead to even higher ROCE. A good rule of thumb is that ROCE should be at least twice the level of underlying interest rates, but in these days of very low interest rates it would be wise to compare yourself against others in your industry and aim to better them.

Your financial position is of course critically important. I like to define a strong financial position as one where you have fairly valued and readily available 'liquid' assets, combined with low amounts of debt when compared to the equity the shareholders have in the business. You can thus service your debt and you have a business that can respond to challenges and capitalise on any opportunities. It's pretty much the same as having a healthy personal financial position.

Now the last point both Peter and I would make is that you need to secure the best management team you can afford, reward them well and ensure that you have good governance standards in place. In other words, the rules, practices and processes used to direct and manage your business. This includes your accounting practices which should be transparent.

When it comes to selling your business, if you are selling for millions of dollars expect to undergo a long and detailed examination by the buyer. They will carry out due diligence checks on you, your fellow directors and your company. I have included a whole section dedicated to this process later in the book. One of the first things I advise start-ups to do is to get their governance and accounting practices right and continue to pay attention to them. This level of discipline will make you run your business well and will ensure at the time you come to sell it, or make it public, the process will be much easier.

Now, I am sure you are thinking that this is a massive and daunting list. Like I said earlier, few companies genuinely tick all these boxes. But if those that you can control early, that cost you little at the start and help you run your business are put in place, such as good governance, then you are not left trying to catch up.

Many of these attributes are simply the sign of a good business. Especially one that wants to be a leader in its industry sector. Developing a position as an industry leader will help you drive superior industry growth.

Keep these in mind as you build and run your business. Aspire to them and measure your strategic plans against the achievement of these attributes and you truly won't go far wrong.

Being clear about valuations and dilution

Those of you who have raised your first funding and are now off and running building your business will probably know all about this, but some of you are just starting out and looking to get their early funding for their first business and will sometimes be confused by some of the terms used and what they mean.

In this section I'm going to talk about pre- and post-money valuations and dilution. These are terms, as an entrepreneur, you need to understand and most importantly understand the implications of.

In truth I see investors confused by this very often. If you don't understand it and don't get it right it can lead to disputes early in the relationship between you and your investors.

So, in simple terms, a pre-money valuation is the

value of a business as it stands now, before any further funds are raised. A post-money valuation is the value of the company after the money has been raised.

It is as simple as that.

In other words, if you all agree that your business is worth two million dollars right now, that is a two-million-dollar pre-money valuation. If you are looking to raise an additional one million dollars to fund your plans, well, after the money is raised your business has a post-money valuation of three million dollars. It is as simple as that.

So, in this example, if a single investor funds your two-million-dollar pre-money valued business by giving you one million dollars, they now own one third of your business. They have contributed one million dollars to a business which now has a three-million-dollar post-money valuation.

If the way you valued your business during your pitch for investors is that it will be worth two million dollars post-money and you are seeking a one million dollar investment, the person funding you to the tune of one million dollars owns half of the business.

It's a simple concept but I have seen pitch decks that talk about values of businesses during a funding round, and they don't say if this is a pre- or post-money valuation. If you are an investor reading this, please correct this and make sure what the basis for the valuation is. It will save you being disappointed.

Of course, it is unlikely that your business will stop trying to raise money to fuel its growth after its first round of funding. You will be looking for a second and probably a third. The same rules apply, when you launch your funding 'round' the former post-money valuation is history. You must establish a new valuation and hopefully it will be bigger than the combined sums of money so far invested. This shows you are creating value for your shareholders.

The logical next thing to discuss is the concept of 'dilution'. This again is a simple concept, but you need to get the maths right and not make assumptions.

Let me try and clarify the way dilution works for you.

In the beginning, if you are the sole founder of your business and therefore own all the shares, you own 100 per cent of your company, and these shares have a value. Maybe it is only the money you put into the company, but it has a value.

As you grow you will start to give shares in your company to people who fund your growth, assuming you are not able to grow organically from sales. You may give shares to employees in exchange for working for you for a below market rate, or you may give some shares to critical suppliers in exchange for their services or reduced prices. It's a way to reduce your cash 'burn'. Every time you give away shares you are diluting your stake in the business.

I have met a lot of founders of businesses who are very reticent about giving away shares in their business for money. I often applaud that, but it is important to realise that money is a resource that your business uses, not just to survive, but to grow. You can of course borrow money from many sources and pay some form of interest on it, but many choose to sell part of their business in exchange for cash that can be used to fund ambitious growth plans. Few businesses get very large without the original founder accepting this form of dilution by selling part of their business.

Think about this. If you can grow your business, beating your competitors in both market share and profit, why would you not use the asset you have built, your business, to secure this?

Let's work an example. If, for example, you own 20 per cent of a company with four other co-founders and the business is valued at 2 million dollars, your stake in the business is worth 400,000 dollars. If your business starts to succeed and you decide you want to raise funds, and you can raise 2.5 million dollars at a pre-money valuation of 7.5 million dollars, your business after the funding round is now worth 10 million dollars post-money. Your stake is diluted by 25 per cent. (2.5 million dollars raised, divided by the 10 million dollars post-money valuation.)

You now own 15 per cent of the business since you accepted a 25 per cent dilution of your share ownership to bring in more funds. In other words, your stake is worth 1.5 million dollars (15 per cent of a business worth 10 million dollars), which is the same as it was when you owned 20 per cent of the business that was valued at 7.5 million dollars. You have created, through business growth and additional funding, a 1.1 million dollar increase in the value of your own investment and the business has gained 2.5 million dollars of cash to use on the next stage of its growth. Therefore, dilution isn't always the evil that some founders seem to think it is.

Dilution is useful to take advantage of opportunities.

Now, it is likely as a start-up or growth company that you will be engaged in multiple rounds of dilutions, and as these grow the situation becomes more complex. It is why careful planning of share ownership is key right from the start. Understanding how you are likely to be diluted over time as either a founder or an investor is critically important. Although it remains true that a 5 per cent stake in a company worth 100 million dollars is significantly more than a 20 per cent stake in a business worth 10 million dollars, there are many other things to consider. Such as your ability to influence the strategy, values and operation of the business you founded.

They are only investors after all

A great business 'guru' that I have a lot of time for and consider a friend, is a guy called Geoff Burch. Check out his books and read a few, the effort will be very worthwhile. You can also find a lot of his presentations on YouTube. Geoff is a real specialist in sales and tells some great stories.

One of the things Geoff does is cut through the corporate babble and get down to what is important. He does it very well and I recall a story he told about the day he went with a senior sales guy to a prospect. When Geoff asked the sales guy what the purpose of their visit was, the sales guy spoke about relationship building and meeting and coming together and all those lovely things, but never once spoke about selling anything to him. Geoff's reaction on stage to that comment is a sight to enjoy, but that's for another time.

It did remind me, though, about the way some founders treat their investors. They seem scared to talk to them. They seem scared to get the best from them. They seem scared to tell stories that contain any bad or less than stellar news at all... until it is too late. If you have followed my advice and really have only taken 'smart money' in funding your early stage business, then you are frankly, by avoiding hard conversations, stifling yourself.

Think about it. These are people who you have worked hard to find, who have bought into your story and vision and probably have been in your industry or something close to it. Do they expect the course of your business to be perfect sailing? I'm sure theirs wasn't. I know mine wasn't. The first dot-com business I led was in the year 2000, a fraction before the dot-com bubble burst. The next one was just starting to grow when the financial crisis of September 2008 hit. It was a business-to-business SaaS offering, with a strong consulting component. What do you think happened to our revenues when every company in the world decided to outsource nothing and hold onto its cash like it was its very lifeblood, because it was?

Now those were big events, but we had many others that caused a few pivots, required some additional funding and a degree of patience from the investors. You will too. Investors expect that. In fact, I get suspicious when companies I invest in are either very quiet, or only ever tell me great news.

So, if you as a founder take nothing from this book other than the message that you should not lie to your investors, then I will consider my work a success if you change your ways. In fact, by lying to your investors you are simply often delaying the inevitable. Now, in this world lying is not just embellishing the truth, it is, in my view, also not communicating issues and problems that will cause the company problems. Lies by omission are still lies.

If you have a character that is likely to lead you to behave in this way, I suggest you don't try and start a business on which your wellbeing depends. Work for somebody else and do a good job and get paid a decent salary with a pension instead.

So just how should you treat investors?

Well point one is recognise that they indeed want your business to succeed just as much as you do. They have trusted you with their money, why would they want you to fail?

Of course, it is easier to tell good news stories, but you must tell the bad news ones as well. Your investors are most likely to be the people who can help you out of the mess you find yourself in. They will have the experience, the contacts and access to the resources you need to address the issue. I know if I find myself sitting in a plane at 30,000 feet, with two incapacitated pilots I want the first call on the intercom to be 'Is there anybody onboard who has commercial piloting experience' and I want that call to be made when I'm still at 30,000 feet in the air, not when the plane is breaking the sound barrier at 1,000 feet from the ground in a vertical dive.

So why then do founders only decide to communicate

with investors when they are two weeks away from running out of cash? If it is a mechanism by which you think you can panic investors into finding more funds to keep you going, well I have news for you. That may work once, you won't get a second chance to 'pull that stunt'.

The real message is don't surprise your investors. Keep them informed of what is going on. Of the five companies I invest in right now, two are brilliant at handling investor communications. Once a quarter they supply me with a newsletter electronically that gives me a 'warts and all' view of their business. When they have a problem they think I can help with, they ring me and get free consultation because I am looking after my investment. Two of them are frankly awful. They don't even supply me with a copy of their annual accounts. Not surprisingly the two companies who communicate with their investors well, in a timely and useful manner, are the ones who are growing profitably, and I am sure will result in my investments paying dividends. If in a few years' time the founders of those companies want me to invest in another new venture they have, I will. The others, well I probably won't even answer their calls.

A key message is, therefore, if you fear having hard but constructive conversations with people who a few months before were strangers to you, then don't build a business that is going to rely on investment other than your own.

If you have investors, get to know their strengths and areas of expertise, and as I have said earlier, contact them one to one when you need help or advice. Trust me, investors do not read everything companies send to them, so if you need help from an investor phone them or email them and ask for it. It is not a sign of weakness, it's a sign of strength.

Finally, find some means of keeping your investors updated, maybe with a short news briefing every three months that lets them know what is going on and how you are doing compared to your business plan and the goals you set. Once a year hold an investor meeting and invite them to attend, it needn't be a lavish affair, in fact it is better that it is not. Invite them to your HQ and share openly what is going on and how you see the future. Keep them engaged and informed, that way when you need help, and you will, it will be there for you.

Getting ready to sell, the need for a company book

When the time comes to sell your business, you need to be ready, and this form of disposal is the most common way people exit their business. This does not mean that you must have the brochures ready for penthouses in Monaco, it means you must make your business as attractive as possible to potential acquirers.

The advice I always give to founders who want to exit via a trade sale, is simply to run your business well. Use good governance principles and keep accurate and substantial accounts.

Most acquirers are looking at your future earnings potential, although of course some will be buying you to 'roll up' the market they are in and eliminate competition. Either way, the decisions you make as you run your business will reflect on the buyer's view of you when they are negotiating with you, or indeed conducting a due diligence review of you. For example, are you paying yourselves, as the founders, a proper salary? How are you using the earnings your business is creating? Are you reinvesting them into the business or taking them as profit or dividends? Each of these approaches sends signals to potential buyers depending upon their own perspective. My advice is always run your business 'in balance'. Pay proper salaries to all staff, including the founders, reinvest well to grow your business and take dividends, or pay them to shareholders when it is appropriate to do so.

A good thing to do, at least a year before you want to start selling your business is to create a company book that is kept up to date and can be handed across to a potential buyer or used by an agent you employ to help you find a buyer. You will find adopting this approach and keeping the information updated will also help you during the due diligence part of any sale.

As a bare minimum I suggest the following things should be in your company book:

- Copies of the company charter documents, shareholders agreements or articles of association including your company registration documents.
- A copy of any shareholder agreement, including any share dealing activities that have taken place both internally and externally.
- A copy of the latest strategy document and financial plans.
- Annual and quarterly financial statements. Annual reports, including your auditor's comments.

- Copies of any patents or applications for patents, trademark filings and awarded trademarks. Include any licencing agreements you have granted or are using.
- A list of the top twenty customers and what proportion of your sales revenues each one represents.
- A list of the top twenty suppliers or subcontractors you buy goods or services from and what proportion of your spend each represents.
- Copies of any contracts over a significant dollar amount relating to purchases made by the company. This would depend upon your size, but I would suggest any contract with spend above 10,000 USD per year as a starting point.
- Copies of any loans, guarantees or other financial instruments the business is currently using or benefiting from.
- An organisation chart of the managers within the business and their relationships to each other and areas of responsibility. For the most senior executives within the business include short biographies and CVs.
- Outlines of any litigations the company has been involved in in the past or are engaged with now.
- Proof of compliance with all required tax activities in each country in which you operate.
- A copy of the current marketing strategy document.
- Copies of all board meeting minutes.
- Copies of all insurance documents pertinent to the company and the individuals working for it.

- Copies of your ESG policies and any permits, licences or legal activities relating to this aspect of your business.
- If appropriate, any written agreements you have as a business with any unions, workers associations or works councils.
- Copies of leases or deeds relating to any properties the company owns or rents.

This information will not only form a significant part of your sales armoury when the time comes, but it will form part, and I do mean only part, of the information that will be required of you once you have agreed to sell your business and the initial price has been agreed. The phase after that will be due diligence on your business being carried out by the organisation that is engaged and is then seeking to buy your business.

Just what is due diligence?
Several people have asked me what they should expect when they have agreed the price to sell their business and the buyer then asks to conduct 'due diligence' on the company as part of the purchase process.

The answer is 'expect to be involved in a great deal of intense, time bounded and detailed work that will consume hours of your senior management teams time and can be very frustrating'. The good news is it feels great when it stops, and the sale then progresses.

So, what does due diligence involve?

Let's go back a step and talk first about what you need to put in place to manage a due diligence process.

When you are selling your business, I strongly advise you to appoint the best solicitor/law firm that you can. Ensure they have experience in helping people sell their businesses. It's a specialist skill set and especially if you are selling to a buyer who is not in your own country, then they need to have experience of international transactions.

Apart from advising you first to get your own people who are directly involved in the sale to sign a specific non-disclosure agreement, they will help the process by setting up an electronic 'deal room'. This is what it says it is. It is a place where all the documents that are requested by the buyer are lodged in files, under electronic locks that you have the control over. It is a place where the buyer can examine these documents, ask questions of them and you and where they receive their answers. It is a secure place where there is a 'single truth'. No documents related to the sale should be passed to any party directly. Every request and every document should only be in the deal room. Any changes or new documents added to the deal room should trigger an email notification to the opposing law firm. Your lawyers will then work with you and your staff to construct and ensure that what is required is there, and they will work with you to make sure it is both complete and correct.

In some cases, it is a matter of simply placing documents in the deal room in the right 'filing cabinet' for your buyer to examine. Things such as your company registration document, or insurance policies fall into this category.

In other cases, the documents and information you lodge will be subject to fierce scrutiny, and in my experience your company financial reports and accounts fall into this category. If, for example, you are a privately held company selling to a quoted or public company, you should expect that your accounts will need to be in a format that the regulatory authorities of the company buying you is registered in. For example, if you are selling to a USA-based company you are almost certainly going to be asked to present your accounts in GAAP format (Generally Accepted Accounting Principles). Do not assume that all accountants you employ are physically capable of doing this or helping you with it. It is no simple task to find accountants who can help you with such transitions and it could cost you significant funds before the deal closes. If you are selling to a business in your own country and you have followed you own countries equivalent to GAAP this should be less of a problem but expect the buyer to expect your accounts to be presented in a way they find acceptable, and you may have to go back and rework a number of years' accounts.

Incidentally, one of the other things that you may have to do is to restate your revenues to truly reflect revenue recognition. It is not uncommon for small businesses not to do this. They often recognise revenue at the time that cash is paid to the business. Proper accounting principles dictate that although the cash for an annual contract may be paid into your bank account at the start of the service being provided, in your P&L account the revenue should only be recognised as the service is delivered. In the case of an annual contract for a software licence for example, this should be in each month during the whole of the annual contract term.

There are many other considerations the buyer will scrutinise involving your finances. Here are just a few of the typical ones:

- Are your accounts audited and to what level, how long have they been subject to an audit?
- What, if any, loans do the company have and what are their exact terms? Copies of the loan agreements will be asked for and examined.
- Are all other liabilities the company has fully declared? Both those that are current and any that are contingent.
- The buyer will seek to determine the aging of your accounts receivable as part of their review.
- Expect to be challenged on the way that working capital is calculated in your financial statements since there are several definitions of working capital and they can lead to differing numbers.
- The buyer is likely to want to see your budgets and financial plans for the coming year at the very least. They may even seek to review your company performance against previous years' plans. If the buyer is examining your current plans in this way, you should expect that the final deal price may be contingent upon performance against this plan. At the very least the buyer will be forming their own view on the likelihood of the company achieving this plan.
- The buyer will seek to determine any capital purchases that need to be made to achieve this

plan and they will want to know about any capital commitments that have already been made.

- Does the company have adequate finances to continue to operate through until when the deal is likely to close?

Depending on your industry, sector, or geography, there are likely to be several other financial considerations your buyer will wish to investigate as part of this due diligence process. Be prepared to dedicate a considerable portion of your time to managing this part of the process.

In terms of intellectual property, the buyer will expect to see and examine any patents and applications for patents that your company has. These can represent considerable value and may well be one of the driving reasons for their interest in your business. Make sure that these have been filed and managed correctly and any associated documents are readily available. By the same token, if you have been subject to any patent infringement claims you should be prepared to present all documentation associated with these claims, even if they are clearly the subject of a 'patent troll' by a company looking to benefit from your unwillingness to defend your own position. Honesty is the key here; it is better to be open than have something you have dismissed or trying to conceal revealed. It is also essential to reveal any times that you have had to defend your patents against others, either currently or in the past.

The data room will need to contain any trademarks that you hold and have filed and had approved. The same is true of any ongoing registrations for trademark registration you have filed anywhere in the world. Again, trademarks can represent significant value and the buyer will want to be assured that your trademarks are both genuine and protected. Once again, you should reveal any litigation either by you or against you involving these trademarks.

Where you either own or use copyrighted materials or products, details of these must be declared.

If you have entered into non-disclosure agreements with any third party, be it a company or an individual, copies of these agreements should also be lodged in the data room. A significant piece of advice here is make sure that all these documents have been fully executed and that it is these copies that are contained in the documentation in the data room. This proves you are taking steps to protect the intellectual capital of your business.

You should declare and reveal any licences that exist between you and other third parties for products, goods, or services that you either licence yourself, or licence to others. Details of these contracts duly executed must be shared with the buyer. You may be asked to evaluate how critical these licences are to your continuing operations and profitability or the earnings generation capabilities of your business. Reveal any contract details that confer any form of exclusivity in your licencing arrangements. When considering this you should also reveal if you have incorporated or use 'open source' software into the operations, technology, or products of your business. Be prepared to have these arrangements investigated.

About software that you use: copies of all licences to operate that software, and proof of your compliance with these licences, needs to be revealed to the buyer.

If there are any other encumbrances, liens, disputes, or indemnities associated with your intellectual property, these should be documented and revealed inside the data room for the buyer to examine and form their own judgements upon.

Now to those people that you trade with or buy or sell services to or from in any way. It is wise to always operate based on contracts and these contracts will form another key element of the information you will be required to lodge in any deal room. I have listed here some of the common examples, but you should review your operations and add to the deal room submissions anything you think will be materially important in closing this sale of the business.

All customer and supplier contracts should be made available, and these include not only the goods and services you buy, but any leasing agreements or rental agreements. If you have any guarantees, loans, equity finance or credit agreements these should be included as well.

Should you operate any form of franchise, the agreements and obligations of these must be made available, as should the details and contracts of any formal partnerships or joint ventures the company is engaged in. The same is true of any dealership, joint marketing, advertising and sales agency agreements.

If you operate any form of exclusivity or 'best terms' agreements or contracts, these should be highlighted, and if you trade with some of the major corporate clients, you should recognise that their contracts may include the right to buy your company as well, or at least be included in any bidding process for the business. This is especially true if you are considered a key supplier to them or an essential component of any production or technology aspect of their business.

If you have a workforce that is represented by a union, then your agreements with the union should be part of your deal room submission and it is not unlikely that a buyer will want to review some or all your current employment contracts between you and your staff.

We are now only part way through what will be expected of you when you are subject to a comprehensive due diligence investigation by a potential buyer.

Let us now go on to discuss the details you are likely to be asked to reveal about your customers, your sales and your employees.

When buying your business, the buyer will have a reasonable idea of your market and customer base but during due diligence they will probe further. You should be prepared to open your books with respect to your customers and at the same time check the content of any customer contracts to ensure that you can do so without gaining their permission. This can be particularly sensitive for your customers if you are being acquired by a competitor.

The information you are likely to be asked for includes revealing who your top twenty or thirty customers are by revenue and margin. At the same time, you would be wise to highlight any problem areas with customers, such as any invoicing disputes, any that you have any form of warranty with and those that are consistent 'late payers'.

There is a possibility that the buyer of your company, especially if they are a competitor of yours, may not be acceptable to a current customer and therefore the buyer will be taking a risk of this customer seeking to take their business elsewhere. You should be sensitive to this and, where appropriate, engage with your existing customer to try and ensure their continued business. Sometimes I have known potential buyers of businesses ask to speak to a selection of customers on a one-to-one basis to judge the level of support and satisfaction they have with your business.

If your business is seasonal, you should also reveal this to your potential buyer, although it should be clear from your cash flow statements it may not be from your profit and loss accounts, especially if you are a business that operates on an annual subscription or licensing model.

Whilst revealing details of your customers, your potential buyer will no doubt also ask to examine sales force compensation models that you operate and ascertain what bonus schemes, if any, are in place and what is the current company obligation to pay any outstanding bonus sums to the sales team.

This brings us onto the information regarding your employees that a buyer will ask to be revealed and will wish to examine.

There is little doubt that the buyer will want to examine and understand details of the salaries, bonuses, pensions, any loans made, or non-cash incentives or benefits that have been made or due to be paid to company directors, officers, or key employees. It is likely that you will need to provide this information for up to six years in the past and for the coming financial year.

You will be expected to provide a summary of other employee benefits, pensions, and proof that provision has been made for these. If you operate a share purchase scheme, provide share options, or have any other agreement with your employees that materially impact ownership of the company, such as 'ghost shares', they should be revealed and documented at this time.

Your employment manuals and any policy documents should be made available for examination, and you should be able to provide documentary evidence that any disputes have been handled in line with these. In addition, you should provide proof to the buyer that all taxes and payments related to your employees have been paid and that you comply with local laws in this respect in all countries in which you operate. If you employ contractors, you will be required to prove that these individuals have been handled in the correct manner for tax purposes and within the legal framework of the countries they have been working in for you.

If, during the last three years, you have been involved in any form of labour dispute with your employees these should be documented and revealed, and any settlements and agreements made should be revealed and documented.

In many countries employees of companies that are being acquired by another benefit from protection of employment legislation. Where this is the case, this should be revealed. If this is not the case then expect to be involved in a discussion regarding the costs and likelihood of any restructuring, layoffs or redundancies after the acquisition is complete.

Although due diligence may already seem a tiresome burden at this stage, we are only part of the way through. Next, we will talk about the information and documents related to your corporate governance and relationship with the authorities that your buyer is likely to be interested in.

During your business operations, you will have most certainly dealt with several regulatory authorities and governments. Where you operate in more than one country, the following will apply to each country in which you have done business or potentially employed individuals.

Due diligence in these areas can be time consuming and difficult. You cannot assume that your potential buyer is familiar with the intricacies of the way your business operates and will therefore be seeking to understand as much as possible what unintentional traps and barriers there may be waiting for it when it buys your company. Because of this I advise companies to over communicate and share information in these areas with buyers.

Typically, there are five areas that will need concentrated effort and patience during due diligence. These are taxation, litigation, competition legislation, insurance and corporate governance. I will take each of these in turn.

Regarding tax you should make available all your

company tax returns in each country in which you operate for a minimum of six years, or whatever term the tax authorities of each country are legally able to review. If you have been subject to any governmental audits the documentation associated with these, and the conclusions, should be revealed.

Any operating losses that are subject to being carried forward or reclaimed must be revealed even if there may be some doubt that these will still be applicable after the sale of the business. The same is true of any tax benefits available from R&D activities or similar benefits provided by the countries in which you operate.

Where you trade between group companies you should detail the transfer pricing arrangements you have in place and provide any correspondence regarding this with local tax authorities.

Tax is a highly complex aspect of your business, and it is here that often your own accountants and auditors will be working closely together as a subgroup of the due diligence process to ensure that everything that needs to be revealed, examined and discussed is completed to the satisfaction of both parties.

The buyer will certainly seek an overview of any litigation your company is currently involved in, or has been in the past. This will include any current filings, or those that have been settled. It will include any court judgements and the documentation associated with these.

If any of these matters have been covered using any form of insurance, such as patent disputes, then detail of these sums, insurance providers, fees and payments should be made available to the buyer.

If any matters involving your business are subject to arbitration or some other form of non-court settlement, these should also be revealed.

Again, it may be that the buyer's legal team seeks access to your own legal firm and advisors to follow up on any issues they discover or have concerns about. You will be required to give your permission for this to happen.

If your buyer is a competitor, the acquisition could be subject to external examination by competition authorities. You should be prepared for this and be willing to contribute fully to the investigative process. The same is true if you work in a regulated industry where external bodies may require examination of the impact of the resulting purchase of your company.

It is important that you reveal to the buyer if you have been subject to any form of anti-competitive or regulatory investigations and the results of these.

It is unlikely that you will be involved in areas such as these, but you could be, and you should allow the time it will take, above that of due diligence for the necessary approvals to be sought and permitted.

Somewhat easier to address, but equally as important to the buyer, will be to have sight of any insurance arrangements or policies you have in place. Examples of these may include general liability, health, key man, car and travel, workers compensation, director and employee liability, patent, intellectual property and indeed any significant risks that you choose to leave uninsured or self-insure.

Several types of corporate documents should be made available and placed in the deal room for examination by the buyers.

I always instruct all businesses that I advise to keep accurate and complete minutes of board meetings. These should include both a list of actions agreed and the results or completion of these activities. This demonstrates a leadership team which is in control and is thorough in its dealings. Even when no meetings have taken place there should be written records of agreements made and the consents given by directors.

A shareholder's agreement should be in place and a register of all shareholders should be current and accurate. This should include details of share ownership, warrants, options, or preferred shares.

I have previously mentioned all corporate documents associated with the existence and establishment of the company. These should also be placed into the deal room for inspection and examination by the buyer.

Similar to this, the buyer will wish to assure itself that your company has been operating legally with respect to any permits, licences and other regulatory issues in all of the countries in which it operates or trades. All documentation associated with these items should also be made available and placed into the deal room.

If you have made it through to this part of my dialogue on due diligence, congratulations. Trust me, reading this is nowhere near as much effort and pain as you will experience if you are part of any due diligence process. Having been part of a number of these I always go into them full of dread, knowing that all the work could end up being for nothing if a deal fails. But most entrepreneurs are aiming to produce a business that is eventually made public or is sold. Due diligence is just part of the journey and, in truth, the work done is never wasted. It can be picked up, updated, and reused, most of it in fact is part of the establishment and daily operations of your business anyway.

So, the last few items I want to talk about that you should be prepared for in the due diligence process are that of your marketing activity and the measures you use to control the products or services that your business provides.

Not all buyers will be deeply interested in this facet of your business, but those who are typically ask to see a copy of your latest marketing plan. The document that matches your company strategic plan but focusses on how you market your business and what your 'go to market' strategy is.

Many will want to see the last few years' press releases and market surveys that you have conducted or purchased using third parties. Some potential buyers will ask to speak with the marketing agencies you use, assuming you do, and will look at your measures of spend versus effect, especially if you are heavily involved in digital marketing. You may in fact discover that the buyer has already had their own digital marketing agency review your activities and spend and have already formed their own judgement on ways they could increase the effectiveness of your marketing.

Finally, expect to share your company literature, price lists and any other associated marketing documents especially those that are part of partnership arrangements or even joint ventures.

If you are a manufacturing business that holds inventories you should expect that your inventory figures, outstanding orders, or any backlog will be investigated, including at one point a physical count of your inventory. This will include not just your finished stock and work in progress but those components and raw materials that are supplied to you for you to create your products. This will extend to any inventories held on your behalf by your suppliers.

Many buyers, when reviewing the purchase of a company that produces goods for sale, or for retail, will ask to examine and understand the control mechanisms you use to run the business. Things such as outputs or throughputs will be reviewed. If you are a service business, then expect to have your staff efficiency reviewed and examined. Very often you will be asked to show your records to support the numbers you are presenting.

Many manufacturing businesses have a significant environmental impact as well, and it is not uncommon for your environmental policies to be reviewed by a buyer. This will not just examine your use and handling of hazardous, regulated or licenced materials you use in the course of your business, but your plans to reduce your impact upon the environment and any commitments that have been made by your business.

In conclusion, due diligence is a time consuming process that will involve people inside and outside your business.

One of the things the deal room should contain is a

comprehensive and updated disclosure document. This document details everything that you have or are planning to add to the data set in the deal room. The buyer will want to see this first so that they can review it and decide if there are clearly other things they wish to see, as well as those you have detailed in the disclosure document. The disclosure document is a living entity that will reflect everything that is added to or removed from the deal room and getting it right is one of the keys to having a due diligence process that runs smoothly and effectively.

As a seller of a business, you should expect that, as the deal closes, the buyer will ask you for warranties. These allow claw backs or sums to be paid to the buyer after the deal closes to assure them that the information you have provided is accurate. They are also put in place at times if there are regulatory or tax matters that could be subject to interpretation.

Remember that the buyer of your business, having agreed a price with you, can modify their offer based upon what they discover as they go through the due diligence process. I have seen some buyers use the process to actively drive agreed prices downwards, but not often. You should be aware that it does happen, and I would strongly advise any seller to make sure that in all discussions with the buyer you act swiftly, openly and honestly. If you have been less than honest the due diligence process will find you out. It is after all one of the reasons that buyers insist on it.

Finally, many of you will sell your businesses without having to go through such a comprehensive due diligence process as I have described in these last pages. But some of you will be exposed to an even greater scrutiny than those I have described here. You are always at liberty to refuse or question the need a buyer has for the information they are asking for but remember when due diligence is taking place you are still in the negotiation phase of the deal.

The book is now at its end. I hope you have enjoyed reading it and have learnt a few things. If that is the case, then I am happy, and hopefully what I have shared with you will prove valuable.

Never once have I mentioned one other essential element that people who start, run, and grow businesses need. That is passion. You must be passionate about your idea, such that other people see that passion and want to be part of the journey with you. Remember, the best salespeople are passionate about what they are selling. It comes across when they talk. When you first start, you are selling the invisible, a promise, an idea, an invention that others need to buy into. Succeed by keeping it simple and by showing your passion for your ideas.

Good luck, and start thinking what you will do with the money you make.

ABOUT THE AUTHOR

Garry Mansell has over 40 years' experience in procurement, supply chain management and latterly as an entrepreneur. During the last twenty years he has built two businesses. The first of which was called Freight Traders. It launched at the height of the dot-com boom in 1999 and became one of the leading freight exchanges in Europe. In 2006 he led the merger of Freight Traders with the embryonic Swedish business Trade Extensions. During the next ten years, as CEO he led the business to its position as the undisputed leader in the field of sourcing optimisation, before initiating and managing its sale to Coupa Software.

Since then, he has invested in and worked as a non-executive director and board advisor with several small and medium-sized businesses operating in areas as diverse as digital marketing, healthcare, animal nutrition, artificial intelligence and machine learning.

He is a fellow of the Chartered Institute of Logistics and Transport and a Fellow of, and Global Board Trustee of, the Chartered Institute of Procurement and Supply.